Coding for Kids

A Hands-on Guide to Learning the Fundamentals of How to Code Games, Apps and Websites

---

Elliot Davis

Contents

INTRODUCTION 6

CHAPTER 1: FUNDAMENTALS OF CODING 9

1.1 Perks of Learning Coding 10

1.2 Basic Coding Terminology..15

1.3 Types of Coding Languages 23

CHAPTER 2: CREATING YOUR 1ST WEBPAGE WITH
HTML & CSS.. 34

2.1 HTML Fundamentals 34

2.2 CSS Fundamentals 42

2.3 Creating a Basic Webpage 58

CHAPTER 3: MAKING YOUR WEBPAGE INTERACTIVE
THROUGH JAVASCRIPT 77

3.1 JavaScript Fundamentals 77

3.2 Adding Functionality to Webpage 106

CHAPTER 4: CODING FOR PONG 118

4.1 HTML Code for Pong 119

4.2 CSS Code for Pong 121

4.3 JavaScript Code for Pong 121

4.4 Results of Pong...132

CHAPTER 5: CODING FOR ROCK, PAPER, AND SCISSORS
.... 134

5.1 HTML Code for Rock, Paper, and Scissors 134

5.2 CSS Code for Rock, Paper, and Scissors 136

5.3 Java Script Code for Rock, Paper, and Scissors 136

5.4 Results of Rock, Paper, Scissors 138

CHAPTER 6: CODING 4 SNAKE 140

6.1 HTML Code for Snake 140

6.2 JavaScript Code for Snake 142

6.3 Results of Snake 144

CHAPTER 7: CODING FOR TIC TAC TOE 145

7.1 HTML Code for Tic Tac Toe 145

7.2 CSS Code for Tic Tac Toe 147

7.3 JavaScript Code for Tic Tac Toe 154

7.4 Results of Tic Tac Toe 166

CHAPTER 8: CODING FOR DINOSAURS 168

8.1 CSS Code for Dino 168

8.2 JavaScript Code for Dino 170

8.3 Results of Dino 175

CHAPTER 9: CODING EXERCISE – TEST YOURSELF 177

9.1 HTML Exercises 177

9.2 CSS Exercises..179

9.3 JavaScript Exercises 181

CONCLUSION.. 183

Leave a Review

Reference pages

Introduction

Did you know that 71% of all the new jobs in Science, Technology, Engineering, and Mathematics (STEM) are in computing, but the Computer Science graduates in STEM are appallingly limited to 8%? Did you know that only 1% of the US population knows how to code? Do not these stats tell you that there is an amazing career opportunity for your children, and they can definitely benefit from it?

One day, I was munching on my pancakes in a café, and I got intrigued to see my elderly neighbor struggling with something on his laptop two benches from me. I went to offer help and saw him having some coding lessons. When I inquired about the problem, he told me that his computer-inquisitive granddaughter was coming over, and he wanted to teach her coding to spend interactive time with her. I volunteered to help, and that was one happy grandfather on his way to meet his granddaughter.

That day, I came upon the realization that coding is still new to people, and there is a lot of vagueness around the subject. As grandparents and parents, we went to school learning everything we felt we would ever need to know, and coding was not one of them.

And coding is still not taught in most schools for kids and teenagers today. Learning to code is not accessible in many schools for a number of reasons, like school budget constraints, a shortage of teaching resources, curriculum inflexibility, and more.

All of this unfamiliarity makes the subject look like a devil and is stealing a big chance for children to prosper. This field not only provides a competitive advantage but can also help children improve their creativity, problem-solving, persistence, collaboration, and communication.

Now, I understand the challenges a beginner might face while learning to code, might you be a parent, grandparent, or a kid, as it is new to all of you. Believe me, I have gone through it all because I was a beginner myself once.

You must be trying to understand it all at once and then getting confused by all abstract ideas and terms. Coding is almost like learning a whole other language, so it is supposed to be tricky. Second, it must be taking you a lot of time, and you will be getting frustrated by it. As a parent, it must be really hard for you to take time out, and as for the young children here, your ambitiousness and the urge to learn everything quickly can be taking a toll on your mind. Thirdly, you might be finding it challenging to apply the theoretical knowledge to solve your coding problems. And the reason which will be contributing to all of the above is the availability of helpful content on the internet. The Internet is no doubt a blessing, but the amount of information on it can sometimes be extremely overwhelming and also misguide and confuse you.

Now take a deep breath because all of your troubles will be gone with this one book. You will have all the data at one place that you need to learn for basic coding, and that will be enough knowledge for you to develop games of your own.

I have a passion for coding, and my experience with coding goes back five years. I have taken more than ten courses in coding to improve my expertise over the years. I have failed plenty of times along the way to know what hurdles beginner coders may experience on their ventures and have found the best practices to deal with these problems.

This book is an honest effort in the face of the alarmingly low interest and skill in the coding field in spite of being such a promising way of securing your future. I have divided the book into nine chapters in an attempt to make it easy and detailed for you. In the first three chapters, you will understand the fundamentals of coding, and in the next four, you will code games for practice. In the last chapter, I have compiled some exercises for your practice.

The first chapter will discuss the crux of coding and what benefits you can achieve from learning this skill. I will include the basic terminologies related to coding and the top five coding languages and their brief descriptions, i.e., JavaScript, Java, HTML, Python, CSS. You will also get to know which language is the best to use in which circumstances with examples.

The second chapter will be a step-by-step guide devoted to creating a basic webpage. Here you will understand the basics of HTML and CSS and learn how they both work together. By the end of this part, you will have a basic webpage with text and images.

The third chapter will all be JavaScript-related to enhancing your webpage. You will learn the basics of JavaScript like object-orientated programming, strings, Booleans, variables, constants, dynamic typing, arrays, functions, etc. I will quote the real-world application of Java Script on a professional level. Lastly, you will get a grasp of coding in JavaScript along with the knowledge of different web languages that interact together to make a webpage.

The following five chapters will be dedicated to coding kids' games like Tic Tac Toe, Pong, and Snake one by one meticulously.

At the end of the book, you will find practice exercises for HTML, CSS and JavaScript.

Now you are more than welcome to begin this easy, thoroughly detailed "coding book" specially designed for children.

Chapter 1: Fundamentals of Coding

Coding powers the world as we know it, but the majority of people are unaware of its nature. Let alone what it is, the fact is that coding is essential for the majority of modern businesses.

Our digital world is propelled by code. Every website, mobile app, computer program, calculator, and even microwave rely on coding for their function. As a consequence, coders are the digital age's developers and designers.

In its most basic form, coding is telling a machine what you want it to do by typing in step-by-step instructions for the computer to execute. Computers are not principally intelligent, but they are highly obedient. They will do just what you want them to do if you teach them how to do it properly. Let me tell you a little about how it works:

What is the deal with coding?

A machine can understand only two types of data: off and on. In fact, a computer is nothing more than a series of "off/on" switches i.e. transistors. Anything a computer can do is a one-of-a-kind blend of some switches turned on, and some switches turned off.

These combinations are represented as 0s and 1s in binary code, with each digit representing one switch. Binary code is divided into bytes, which are groups of eight digits that represent eight switches, for example, 11001101. Modern computers produce millions, if not billions of switches, resulting in an unfathomably huge number of potential combinations.

But there is one issue here. To be able to build a computer program by writing billions of 1s and 0s will necessitate superhuman powers, and even if accomplished, it would most likely take you a lifetime or more.

This is why we need programming languages.

We can build computer applications, apps, and websites; thanks to hundreds and hundreds of different programming languages. Instead of binary code e.g. 01010, they allow us to write code that is comparatively simple to read, write, and understand. Every language requires a special program that translates what we add to binary code.

Various languages are designed for specific purposes – some are valuable for web creation, others for making desktop applications, still others for solving numerical and scientific problems, and more.

Programming languages are of two types: low-level and high-level.

Low-level languages find more similarities to the binary code (e.g. 01011) that computers understand, whereas high-level languages are much less similar to binary code. Since they are less complicated and built to be simple for us to write, high-level languages are simpler to program in.

Almost all of the common programming languages in the modern world are high-level languages.

Now, before I get into more basics of coding, let me help you understand how valuable it can be for you:

1.1 Perks of Learning Coding

Many people used to think of coding as a strange hobby for geeks tweaking with machines in their basements. However, coding has evolved from a hobby to a vital career skill over the last few years. Employers have expressed a willingness to pay a premium for workers with coding and programming expertise. That being said, let's have a look at our first advantage:

1. **Earning Profitability:** The earning opportunity for coding and programming professionals is one of the best and most visible draws of learning to code. The Bureau of Labor Statistics (BLS) monitors wage and other significant employment data for a wide range of occupations.

   Take a look at the BLS's 2019 median annual wage data for the following coding and programming-related occupations (keep in mind the average annual wage of 40,000):

   1. $83,510 for network and computer system administrators

   2. $73,760 for web developers

   3. $86,550 for computer programmers

   4. $107,510 for software developers

5. $93,750 for database managers

As you can see, occupations that include certain programming, coding, or scripting skills tend to pay more than the average.

2. **Smarter Perspective:** It has been shown that learning to code will help you do better in other subjects you are studying or learning. Programming teaches you how to divide a problem into discrete steps and use a computer-friendly language to logically construct a functioning program.

> As a result, you develop a particular mindset for approaching problems and processing large quantities of information, which is needed for mastering any new subject. In other words, you learn to look at problems from a broader perspective and adjust to dealing with the frustrations of reaching an obstacle and creating a plan of attack in order to fix problems.

> Coding involves critical thinking and teaches children how to approach complicated problems by breaking them down into smaller, easier-to-manage and solve problems. This is referred to as decomposition. Even if a child cannot become a skilled software engineer or computer programmer, learning to think in this manner is a transferable skill.

> It has been said that learning how to think is more important than learning what to think. Learning to code entails more than just learning a programming language. It entails developing an efficient and constructive attitude toward problem-solving that will benefit any new intellectual venture you undertake.

3. **Job Opportunities:** When it comes to coding jobs, it seems that there is still plenty of availability.

> The following are the most recent BLS forecasts for job growth in the same coding and programming-related professions:

> · 13%: web developers.

> · 5%: Administrators of network and operating systems

- 7%: Computer programmers
- 9%: Database managers.
- 21%: App developers.

When the national average of 5% growth is kept in mind, it is obvious that a small number of jobs are outpacing many others. Computer programmers are an interesting outlier in this community but some claim that this is due to computer programming skills blending into other similar in-demand tech positions.

Although the job remains extremely valuable, an increasing number of hybrid roles are being integrated into the workforce. As a result, there are fewer job listings for "computer programmers" and more openings that incorporate programming expertise with other job titles.

Moreover, using coding as a string to your bow will help you find employment in the industry (like marketing, content creation, PR, and more). Even if you are applying for a job that has nothing to do with coding, it is always a valuable skill to have. As a consequence, merely learning about it would give you an advantage over the competition. Aside from being a generally useful ability in most of the jobs, it also demonstrates that you are dynamic, hardworking, and a self-starter.

4.   **Improved Creativity:** Students may become developers by learning to code. After all, coding is all about inventing new things. What a dream it would be to be able to create your own app or video game. Kids may use code to build projects that they enjoy. Students who learn to code increase their imagination and learn how to come up with their own ideas to solve problems. This is an essential ability that extends well beyond the confines of a machine.

5.   **Strong Resilience:** Resilience is not something that can be taught. As a result, children must gain experience in order to develop this skill. Children learn to develop resilience by troubleshooting, which is a significant advantage of learning to code. When they encounter a problem, they must devise a workable solution. If the first solution fails, they try another. If that does not succeed, they try again and again till the issue is

resolved. In computer programming, it is referred to as debugging. These forms of thinking abilities are in high demand.

6. **Communication Skills:** Coding is almost like learning a new language. Although it is not Spanish or Italian, learning to code requires some of the same skills that we need while learning a new language. We become better communicators when we learn a new language. Why is this so? To speak clearly, we need to know how to break things down. The same is true for coding. Computers can only interpret instructions written in plain, easy-to-understand language that the machine understands. Coding aids in the development of that ability.

7. **Math Skills:** Math skills are needed to learn coding. This does not imply that students must be Mathematical geniuses to learn computer programming. It simply means that when they learn to code, they will acquire the skills needed to solve math problems.

   Learning by playing is the best way to learn, and yes, coding can be enjoyable. Children may not be aware of the skills they are learning when coding. Coding necessitates solving real-world problems rather than completing a worksheet full of math equations, allowing them to obtain real-world knowledge that will help them develop their math skills.

So this book is for anyone who wants to benefit from the above perspectives. I would recommend this book to specifically teenagers who would like an intro into how coding works and how to do basic coding with the thought of expanding and applying their knowledge after they complete this book. I am now going to include some resources which you will find very valuable during your coding ventures:

1. **Codecademy:** This online platform has one of the most extensive course catalogs of any free course provider. The platform has over 25 million learners who are exploring various coding opportunities for free. You can also upgrade it to a Pro account for almost 20$ per month or almost 200$ a year, which unlocks additional features. You can choose from a diverse variety of courses at Codecademy.

2. **Udemy:** This is one of the most well-known e-learning sites in the world. It provides thousands of video tutorials. Although some of them are free, you will have to pay for many of them, with prices ranging from $10 to about $200. Udemy also provides limited-time discounts on courses. It just requires you to sign up for email updates.

3. **EdX.org:** This open-source higher education platform offers a computer science category with around 320 different courses. Furthermore, it has to offer both free and paid courses that range from $50 to $300. You only have to pay for the free courses if you need a certificate to prove the completion.

4. **Lynda:** LinkedIn is the creator of Lynda.com. You can access hundreds of courses and thousands of video tutorials on a wide variety of coding topics through this online learning site. With over 400 software development courses and over 100 web development offerings, you are bound to find the training you need. Lynda.com provides a free trial, after which you can choose between the Simple plan for $19.99 per month. This plan allows you access to the entire library (5,000+ courses), and the Premium plan for almost $30 per month. Premium covers everything in Basic, as well as project files and code practice, quizzes, and offline course watching.

5. **Treehouse:** A treehouse is an excellent option for beginners because it is both enjoyable and easy. To keep learners entertained, the videos include a bit of humor and some engaging development. It charges a monthly subscription fee of $25 for the Basic plan and $50 for the Pro plan. Treehouse offers a free two-week trial period to new users. An additional bonus is the site's freelancing and business strategy tutorials, which will help you put your new coding skills to use.

Now I think you have understood how valuable asset coding can be for you, and you have noted down some resources to help you out with it more. Let's get into further details of coding. But before we go deep into coding functions, I want to let you know about some terms you will continuously hear in the coding world.

1.2 Basic Coding Terminology

Attempting to provide definitions for all the programming languages will necessitate many more pages than I currently have. However, I have put together a list of some of the most popular words you will come across as you begin your coding journey. Let's begin in chronological order.

A

· Algorithm

> An algorithm is a series of instructions for resolving a problem. It is the thinking process of a machine.

· Array

Arrays are variable containers that are used to group together related variables. Arrays are similar to (pet) store racks. The array would be the shelf.

· Argument

An argument is a method of providing additional information to a function. The knowledge can then be used as a variable by the function as it runs.

· Arithmetic Operators

Arithmetic operators, such as "+" for addition, are used with numbers to execute basic math. To do almost everything, computers must add and subtract, multiply and divide.

API

Application Programming Interface contains a set of routines, protocols, and tools for developing software applications. APIs are used to describe software components in terms of their processes, inputs, outputs, and underlying types. In your bootcamp final project, for example, you could use a Google Maps API to build specialized maps by making use of existing geolocation infrastructure.

- **Augmented Reality**

    Augmented reality (AR) is a real-time virtual experience in which digital objects are positioned in a real-world environment.

B

- **Binary Number**

    A binary number is a computer's method of representing data. Computers process millions of 1's and 0's every minute, applying various rules to interpret them as letters, numbers, operators, and everything else that is entered into a machine.

- **Back-end**

    The server side of the development is referred to as back-end development, and the main emphasis is on how the web functions. This is normally composed of three components: an application, a server, and a database. The back-end function is invisible to users, but code written by back-end developers is what communicates database information to the browser.

- **Backbone.js**

    A JavaScript library that provides structure and handles user feedback and interactivity for one-page web apps.

- **Block-Based Programming**

    Block-based programming allows users to build programs by dragging and falling code blocks (as opposed to writing text). For example, scratch is a block programming language.

- **Bit**

    A single 0 or a single 1. In computing and digital communications, it is the smallest unit of information.

- **Bug**

    It is a code that has been disabled and is causing a program to malfunction. Bugs sometimes cause a program to crash or display an error message.

C

- **C++**

    C++ is a simple but powerful programming language. Children who learn this language would be able to solve difficult problems and comprehend how programs function.

- **Compilation**

    It is the process of converting code into a computer-readable format. Compilation is a term used to describe certain programming languages. Before these codes can be used, they must be compiled.

- **Compilation of works**

    It is the process of converting code into a computer-readable format. Compilation is a term used to describe certain programming languages. Before these can be put to use, they must be compiled.

- **Computer Program**

    A computer program is a series of instructions that are given to a computer to be implemented. These instructions are usually used to solve a problem or to shorten and simplify long problems for humans.

- **Conditional Statements**

    Conditional statements are either true or false. In various cases, use them to print information or advance programs.

- **Camel Case**

    A type of capitalization that is used to name variables. The first letter of a word is always lowercase, and the first letter of every subsequent word is uppercase. For example, the word "thisVariable" and "iPhone" is written in camelcase.

- **Cloud**

    A cloud-based data storage facility, such as Dropbox. The word "cloud" applies to general internet storage or facilities.

- **CLI**

    CLI stands for Command-Line Interface. It is a text-based method of communicating with a device. There are no keys, dropdowns, or other items that can be pressed.

D

- **Database**

    A computer database management system is a system for storing and organizing data. Databases are used to facilitate the collection of information.

- **Deployment**

    When all of the tasks that make a software system available for use are completed, reviewed, and ready for users, the software is deployed. You should plan to deploy to a platform like Heroku when attending a coding Bootcamp. Users will access the code after it has been deployed.

- **Defining Function**

    It is to write a function and the code that goes with it. When a function is specified, the programmer will call it when it is required.

- Digital Footprint

  Any details that you leave on a website. A blog post, a comment, or a "like" may all leave a digital trail.

- Django

  Django is a programming language. A web-based Python framework. Django simplifies Python website growth. It is a compilation of templates and libraries.

- **DRY**

  DRY is an acronym that stands for Don't Repeat Yourself. According to this theory, "Every piece of information inside a structure must have a single, unambiguous, authoritative representation."

- **DNS**

  DNS stands for Domain Name System (domain name service.) A computer system that converts a written domain name into a series of numbers. These are referred to as IP (Internet Protocol) addresses. IP addresses are needed for computers to locate websites.

E

- Express.js

  Express.js is a Node.js web app back-end server platform that can be used to build multi-page, single-page, and hybrid web applications. It is the most common Node.js system since it simplifies the process and provides additional plug-ins.

- Event

  An event is something that causes a program to react, such as a mouse click or a button push.

- Event Handler

  Code that reacts to a user-initiated event, such as a mouse click or button press.

F

- **Function**

  A function is a part of code that can be called by name to execute the code it contains.

- **Framework**

  A set of "templates" that programmers use to create programs quickly. Frameworks may include pre-written code, markup, and APIs. There are web interfaces for both the front end and the back end.

- **For Loops**

  For loops allow coders to run a block of code repeatedly.

G

- **Github**

  Github is a Python-based microweb platform where developers can store Git repositories and interact with other developers.

- **Git**

  Git is basically an open-source version control system that is popular because of its data integrity, speed, and support for distributed, non-linear workflows. Consider it a collection of snapshots of your code. Every Git directory on every device contains a complete database with history and full version monitoring, regardless of network connectivity or a centralized server.

H

- **HTTP Request**

  The mechanism by which a web browser requests information from a server. HTTP is an abbreviation for HyperText Transfer Protocol.

I

- ## IDE

  An Integrated Development Environment (IDE) is the platform where you type your code and run your programs. An IDE is essentially a software that simplifies coding.

- ## IntelliJ

  To begin writing Java code, you can use IntelliJ. It is an IDE built for writing and running code.

L

- Local Environment

  The local world, also known as the production environment, is where software updates are made before they are deployed. After testing, the code is moved out of the local environment and into development.

M

- ## Machine learning

  Machine learning is the method of getting a computer to behave without specifically training it to do so. It is an artificial intelligence application in which we give machines access to data and allow them to learn for themselves. Find out more about machine learning for children.

- ## Micro Bit

  The micro bit is a small programmable device that is often referred to as a microcontroller development board.

N

- ## Neural Networks

  Neural Networks are actually computer programs that are designed to mimic the human brain. Neural networks, like humans, learn over time.

-

Null

It means empty or having no value. Variables and columns in a database can be null at times.

- **Node.js**

Node.js is a programming language that helps you to execute JavaScript code outside of a web browser

O

- **Object-Oriented Programming**

A prototype that describes the characteristics of everything that is part of it. A class's members are all objects.

P

- **Program**

Code that is written and executed on a machine. The bulk of systems are made up of user interfaces and logic. Adobe Illustrator is a piece of software. Microsoft Outlook is also a piece of software.

R

- **RESTful**

A set of rules that enables computers to communicate with one another. The world wide web is made possible by REST (Representational State Transfer).

- **Ruby**

Ruby is a formalized paraphrase. Ruby is, in fact, a programming language that has been developed to be readable. It is object-oriented and can be used for a wide range of applications. Ruby was used to creating AirBnB and GitHub.

S

- **Script**

Small systems that take just a few moves. Scripts can be used in broader systems.

- Source Code

  The code was written by programmers that are ultimately converted into applications. A compiler must first convert the source code into machine code.

V

- Version Control

  Software that allows programmers to save several versions of their code. Previous work is not deleted or lost as a result of this. It also assists programmers in keeping track of changes.

W

- While Loop

  A piece of code that repeats itself as long as a certain condition is met. A loop, for example, could run when a certain number is less than 6 and then stop when it reaches 6.

X

- XML

  A markup language that, like HTML, regulates how information appears on a computer. However, XML files can be read and written outside of web browsers.

Mentioned above are some of the coding terms that you will find hard to grasp as a beginner. Moving on, at the start of this chapter, I gave you a brief introduction to programming languages. Now let's discuss the type of programming languages.

1.3 Types of Coding Languages

Today, there are thousands of programming languages available. Coding languages are not like ours in the sense that they lack vocabularies and alphabets. They are more like codes – special instructions, abbreviations, and text-arrangement methods.

Every piece of software is written in some kind of coding language. Every coding language is distinct, having been created with a specific coding style, operating system and for a specific platform. It is designed to perform some specific intended use.

I do not want you to be confused when choosing a programming language to get started, so I am listing the top 5 coding languages with their uses. Let's start:

1. Java

Sun Microsystems developed Java, a high-level programming language. It was originally intended for developing programs for handheld devices and set-top boxes (A system that allows a television to receive and decode broadcasts for digital television), but it quickly became popular for developing web applications. Java is the most popular and common programming language, and it is used to create anything from server-side applications to smartphone applications and video games. It is also the foundation for creating Android apps, so it is a popular choice among programmers.

Java was developed primarily for use in the distributed world of the Internet. It was created with the feel and look of the C++ programming language in mind, but it is easier to use. It also enforces an object-oriented programming model (OOP.) Bjarne Stroustrup founded C++ in 1979. It is a compiled language that can run on a variety of hardware platforms. OOP is a programming type in which you can manage certain objects (like characters in a game) separately without disrupting other objects. In simple words, it changes the spaghetti mess of codes into pizza toppings where you can pick and move one item without a mix-up.

Java can be used to build full applications that can run on a single computer or be spread through a network of clients and servers. It can also be used to construct a small application module or applet (a small, simple application) that can be added to a Web page. Applets enable a Web page visitor to interact with the page. Let me show you some real-world examples.

Java Applications

Java is used in a variety of contexts, ranging from a commercial e-commerce platform to android apps, from science applications to financial applications such as electronic trading systems, from games such as Minecraft to desktop applications such as Netbeans, Eclipse, and IntelliJ, from J2ME apps to an open-source library, and so on.

I am going to discuss a few examples:

- The Android operating system is heavily dependent on Java, and Android phones consistently have a market share of more than 85%. The majority of mobile app developers refer to Java as their official programming language. Java is consistent with software development tools like Kotlin and Android Workshop.

- Java is very popular in the financial services industry. Many global investment banks, including Citigroup, Goldman Sachs, Barclays, Standard Chartered, and others, use Java to build front and back office electronic trading systems, data processing ventures, settlement and confirmation systems, and other applications.

- Science-related mathematical calculations and operations necessitate the development of apps that are extremely fast, easy to maintain, highly stable, and portable. Java meets this requirement admirably. Java is used as part of the core framework and interacting user interfaces in powerful scientific applications such as MATLAB.

- The gaming industry and Java are a perfect fit. The jMonkey engine, one of the most powerful 3D engines available today, is supported by Java. And 2D games are a breeze to create. Simply combine Java and CSS, and you are good to go. So, regardless of the type of game developers are making, Java has them covered.

2. JavaScript

JavaScript is a text-based coding language that can be used on both the client and server sides to render web pages interactive. JavaScript introduces interactive elements to web pages, enabling users to communicate with them. JavaScript is often used in everyday applications such as the Amazon search box, refreshing the Twitter feed, or a news recap video embedded in The New York Times.

JavaScript is a scripting language, and it allows you to create dynamically updating content, monitor multimedia, animate images, and do a lot more. It was created by Netscape but is now used by the majority of web browsers. Since it can communicate with HTML, it enables web developers to include dynamic elements in their websites. It is an open-source programming language, which ensures that anybody can use it without purchasing a license.

Many people feel puzzled by the distinction between Java and JavaScript. They may share a name, but that is where the similarities end:

- Java is a complex and efficient programming language, while JavaScript is a lightweight scripting language.

- Both are OOP-based programming languages, but although JavaScript is a scripting language, Java is an OOP-based programming language.

- Java needs programming language interpreters to translate it to machine language that a computer system can understand. JavaScript is only expected to be interpreted by the browser engine when a webpage is loaded.

- JavaScript needs a client to work. The browser is the device. As a web user, you can choose to disable JavaScript, which will prevent it from working in your browser. Java does not need a client. It designs software that can run on a virtual machine or in a browser.

- Although Java programs behave exactly the same across various systems, the same cannot be said for JavaScript. A JavaScript-created web page behaves differently in different web browsers.

Now let me give you some examples.

JavaScript Applications

JavaScript is much more powerful than it was just a few years ago. Here is a fast rundown of what JavaScript can do:

- JavaScript allows you to add behavior to a web page so that it responds to actions without loading a new page to process the request. It allows the website to communicate with tourists and carry out complex actions.

- As browsers develop day by day, JavaScript has grown in popularity for creating robust web applications. We can understand it better by using Google Maps as an example. In Maps, the user just needs to click and move the mouse to see the details. The details are available with a single click. Behind these ideas is the use of JavaScript.

- JavaScript's features and applications make it an effective tool for developing mobile applications. The React Native JavaScript platform is commonly used for developing mobile applications. We can create mobile applications for a variety of operating systems using React Native. We do not need to write separate code for the iOS and Android operating systems. We need to write it just once and run it on multiple platforms.

- JavaScript is also useful for creating website presentations. Libraries such as RevealJs and BespokeJs can be used to build a web-based slide deck. They are easier to use, so we can easily create something spectacular in a short period of time.

2. HTML

HTML is a markup language that is commonly used to build web pages and web applications. HTML has been a web creation milestone when paired with JavaScript and CSS (a programming language for setting out and structuring web pages). One of HTML's useful features is the ability to insert programs written in a scripting language such as JavaScript, which is responsible for influencing the behavior and content of web pages. HTML components are the fundamental building blocks of all HTML pages. A structured document can be produced using structural-semantic text such as paragraphs, headings, lists, links, and other objects. The HTML tags are not displayed by the browser, but they are used to interpret the page's content. It is important to research various tags in order to comprehend their actions.

HTML is not a programming language, which means that it cannot construct dynamic features. Instead, it allows you to arrange and format documents in the same way as Microsoft Word does.

Now let's get into examples:

HTML Applications

Tim Berners-Lee is widely regarded as the "Father of HTML." Tim proposed a paper called "HTML Tags" in late 1991 as the first available definition of HTML. HTML5 is the most recent edition of HTML. Let's discuss some of the services it has to offer:

- HTML is widely used to create pages that are displayed on the internet. Each page contains a collection of HTML tags, including hyperlinks, which are used to link to other pages. Every page that we see on the internet is written in some kind of HTML code.

- Internet navigation is one of the most significant and innovative applications of HTML. This navigation is made possible by using the Hypertext principle. It is simply a text that links to other web pages or text, and when the user clicks on it, they are guided to the referenced text or website. HTML is commonly used to embed hyperlinks within web pages. A user can easily navigate inside web pages as well as between websites that are hosted on different servers.

- HTML is the language of choice for creating documents on the internet. A web document is divided into three sections: the title, the head, and the body. The details needed to identify the text, such as the title and any other relevant keywords, are included in the head. The title can be seen in the browser's bar, and the body section is the main part of the website that the user can see. Tags are the fundamental formatting tool in HTML. HTML tags are used to design and build all three segments. Every segment has its own set of tags, which are rendered explicitly to keep the head, title, and body definitions in sync.

- At the most fundamental level, queries in HTML applications can be configured to use responsive images. A developer can completely monitor how the user renders an image by using the srcset attribute of the IMG element in HTML and combining it with picture elements. The srcset attribute defines the image URL to use in various cases. Using the IMG feature, you can now load different types of images with varying sizes. Rules can be set with the picture element. We can declare the IMG element with a default source and then include a source for each event.

3. Python

Python is a free and easy-to-learn programming language. Its main characteristics are that it is high-level, dynamically typed, and interpretable. This facilitates error debugging and promotes the rapid creation of application prototypes, establishing itself as the language to code in. Guido Van Rossum created Python in 1989, emphasizing the DRY (Don't Repeat Yourself) concept and readability. The programming language's basic syntax rules make it much simpler to keep the code base readable and the functionality maintainable.

Its functions can be accomplished with fewer commands and less text than most competing languages. This may explain why it is gaining popularity among developers, coding students, and tech companies.

I will not be blowing it out of proportion when I suggest that Python has a slight but important effect on all of our lives. It is one of those hidden powers that can be found in our mobile devices, web searches, and games.

Let me give you some insight into its usage.

Python Applications

Python is a system that sustains cross-platform operating systems, which makes creating applications for it much easier. Python is used to power some of the world's most well-known apps, including BitTorrent, YouTube, and DropBox. Here are some examples of its usage:

- Python can be used to build a wide range of applications, including graphical user interface applications, web applications, software development applications, network programming, science and numerical applications, 3D applications, games, and business applications. It provides an interactive GUI and encourages application creation.

- It has a wide and stable standard library that can be used to build applications. It also allows developers to use Python over other programming languages. The standard library facilitates the use of the various Python modules. Since this module allows you to add features without writing any additional code, the documentation on the Python standard library may be referred to for information on different modules. The standard library documentation is useful when creating any web application, implementing web services, performing string operations, and other usages such as interface protocol.

- Python, as an open-source programming language, will greatly reduce the cost of software creation. You can also use a variety of open-source Python frameworks, libraries, and development tools to reduce development time while increasing development expense. You can also select from a huge option base of open-source Python frameworks and programming tools based on your specific requirements. For example, using robust Python web frameworks such as Flask, Pyramid, Django, Cherrypy, and Bottle can simplify and accelerate web application creation.

- If you have the knowledge to get the valuable information from data, you can take measured risks and increase income. You examine the data you have, conduct operations, and extract the necessary information. Pandas and NumPy libraries will assist you in extracting information.

You can also visualize Seaborn and Matplotlib libraries, which are useful for plotting graphs and a lot more. Python empowers you with the tools you need to be a Data Scientist.

- Python is also employed in the development of interactive games. There are libraries available, such as PySoy, a 3D game engine that supports Python 3, and PyGame, which provides features and a library for game creation. Python has been used to build games such as Disney's Toontown Online, Civilization IV Vega Attack, and others.

4. CSS

CSS is an abbreviation for Cascading Style Sheets, with an emphasis on the term "style." Although HTML is used to organize a web document (defining items like headlines and paragraphs, as well as allowing you to embed video, images, and other media), CSS comes in and defines the design of your document—page templates, colors, and fonts are all determined by CSS. Consider HTML to be the base (every home has one), and CSS to be the aesthetic choices.

CSS stands for style sheet language, and it is used to describe the appearance and design of web pages, including fonts, colors, and layouts. It is primarily intended to distinguish between appearance and content, including formats, colors, and fonts. It can be used in a variety of applications, including large and small screens, as well as printers. It is not influenced by HTML.

Let's get into some examples.

CSS Applications

Web pages were extremely restricted in both type and purpose prior to the World Wide Web Consortium's (W3C) development of CSS in 1996. Early browsers displayed a page as hypertext, which included plain text, images, and links to other hypertext sites. There was no style to speak of, just paragraphs that ran across the page in a single column.

CSS allowed several advances in webpage layout, such as the ability to:

- CSS has played a significant role in the E-Commerce domain. The E-Commerce domain contains a wide range of industries, and CSS has aided the application frameworks, styling and look-views that are used in industries ranging from small to large. CSS styling may be used to explicitly communicate with the e-commerce web. Furthermore, various add-ins and library files that are present can be changed and updated by CSS libraries. They can be used when designing web applications, and the source codes associated with it can be implemented by CSS in the HTML framework to create an e-commerce web platform from the ground up.

- CSS can be used in a variety of ways to build any web-based application or online community, according to the current standards. CSS contains a variety of style sheet frameworks that can be easily applied over here. The style of one's own online community can be created using CSS. There are also numerous add-ons available, which can be implemented by using CSS frameworks to create the feel and look of the web-based community.

- CSS in HTML frameworks is also being used in the creation of social media websites. Facebook applications can be related to the corresponding frameworks. To build the application, HTML client library files can be developed based on CSS stylings and can work with various extensions. These social media-based sites can be linked to systems and used to develop a few changes from the end user's point of view. As a result, CSS styling and upgrading the user interface becomes simpler, which has a direct effect on social media sites.

- CSS is extremely necessary when it comes to website maintenance. It greatly simplifies website maintenance. The CSS file gives the website a more versatile look and feel, and it can be modified in a more convenient way. It also facilitates the modification of HTML formatting and corresponding data items. As a result, website maintenance becomes more convenient from a growth standpoint.

Five coding languages have been mentioned above that will lay the foundation of your basic coding operations. Now for the next two chapters, you will learn how to make a web page through JavaScript, CSS, and HTML.

Chapter 2: Creating your 1st webpage with HTML & CSS

In the introductory chapter, I gave you brief descriptions of the top five programming languages used around the world. In this chapter, we will use only two of them to help you create your very own webpage. HTML will help you build the structure of the webpage, and CSS will help you decorate and style that structure. In the next chapter, JavaScript will assist you in making the webpage functional.

Let me start by giving you a deeper understanding of HTML and CSS.

2.1 HTML Fundamentals

As described before, HTML is an abbreviation for HyperText Markup Language. HTML is the most commonly used markup language for building web pages. The structure of a Web page is defined in HTML.

HTML is made up of a variety of elements. Let me tell you what they are.

HTML Elements

HTML elements instruct browsers on how to display content. HTML elements mark content, such as "this is a heading," "this is a paragraph," "this is a link," and so on.

Consider an HTML element to be a single piece of a webpage, such as a block of text, a header, an image, and so on. HTML tags are used for any element of HTML, and a tag (</h1> or <h1>) is sandwiched between angled brackets like < and >. Elements are described by tags, which with the correct code direct the browser to display them whatever you want. (e.g., they can direct the browser that an element can be a text paragraph or an image.)

Most HTML elements have a closing and opening tag that indicate where the element ends and starts. The closing tag which we write at the end of the code is simply the opening tag preceded by a forward slash (/).

Let me tell you a few things about elements of HTML before diving into the types of these elements.

1. **Element Attributes:** Certain attributes can be applied to HTML elements to change their features and behavior. These attributes find themselves defined within the opening tag. Directly inside HTML, attributes such as width and height for images and rows and columns for text area are useful. However, some attributes have a special significance. They do little on their own but enable us to write additional JavaScript and CSS and link the three pillars. It should be noted that certain elements do not contain any content and therefore do not require a closing tag. Images, for example, need only a "src" attribute ("src" is short for the source to find the image.)

   Attributes are often specified in the start tag (or opening tag) and are usually composed of name/value pairs such as name= "value." In HTML5, there are some attributes that do not consist of value/name pairs but only of the name. These are known as Boolean attributes. Some common Boolean attributes include: disabled, verified, read-only, needed, and so on. On the majority of HTML elements, you can use attributes such as title, id, style, class, and so on. The following section discusses how to use them:

   · The title attribute is used to provide descriptive text about an element or its contents.

   · The id attribute is used to assign an entity within a document a unique name or identifier. This makes selecting the element with CSS or JavaScript easier.

   · The class attribute, like the id attribute, is used to define elements. However, unlike the id attribute, the class attribute does not have to be specific within the text. This implies that the same class can be applied to multiple elements in a text.

   · The style attribute allows you to explicitly define CSS styling rules such as font, color, border, and so on within the product i.e. webpage.

2.   **Nesting Elements:** HTML elements can be nested within each other; that is, one element can contain other elements.

> HTML tags must be nested in the appropriate order. They must be closed in the inverse order of their definition, which means that the last tag opened must be closed first.

Additional Rules: Aside from these, there are some simple rules that all pages of HTML must follow. For instance, the HTML element at the outermost side must be <html>. Similarly, all 'visible' content is placed in the <body>, while all metadata/configuration (information about the page itself) is placed in the <head>

Now let's have a look at some basic HTML elements used while creating a webpage.

1.   **Headings:** Headings are just what their name means. There are six headings in HTML, numbered h1 through h6. Heading 1 (h1) is the largest and most important heading. It indicates that this is the most important text on the list. As we get closer to h6, the importance decreases steadily.

2.   **Paragraph:** Text blocks are represented by the paragraph variable, p. We normally style paragraphs so that there is a good amount of space between them and between the first paragraph and its heading.

3.   **Anchor Link:** In HTML, the anchor element, a, activates HyperText. It will guide you to another page on a different or same website.

4.   **Lists:** Lists are extremely useful for viewing data in either a structured or unordered format. We use <ol> for ordered lists (a list of numbers) and <ul> for unordered lists (a list of bullet points). Each list item is denoted by <li> inside one of these elements.

5.   **Forms:** We fill out forms on the internet all the time. We can accept user input using form elements. Anywhere you see a place to add text, click a button, or toggle a checkbox, there's an HTML form feature in the context. It can be for posting a message or logging into our social media accounts.

6. **Spans and Divisions:** Anything on a website can be visualized as a collection of boxes. As web developers, our task is to organize these boxes so that the whole page looks good on all screens. These boxes contain the text, pictures, and other elements that we see on websites.

These boxes are referred to as spans (span) and divisions (div). Divs and spans do not do something on their own, but we can add stuff to them, such as text and images, and they allow us to place the text and images wherever we want.

Bags are a good example for divs and spans. Bags such as backpacks and handbags are not very useful on their own. Nobody will walk around with an empty backpack. When we store items in them, they become useful because they help us keep things organized. We can think of divisions and spans in this way. They serve as containers for your website's actual functional components.

Now let me introduce you to some of the basic HTML tags.

HTML Tags

These tags will help you in the basic coding of your webpage:

1. **Line Break Tag:** When you use the <br /> element, all code after it begins on the next line. This tag is an example of an empty element. You do not require opening and closing tags as there is nothing between them. There is a space between the characters br and a forward slash in the <br /> tag. If you leave this out, older browsers will have difficulty in making the line split. Moreover, if you miss the forward-slash character and only use <br>. It will not be valid in XHTML.

2. **Centering Content:** You may use the <center> tag to center any material on the page or in a table cell.

3. **Horizontal Lines:** Horizontal lines are used to visually divide parts of a text. The <hr> tag draws a line from the current location in the text to the right margin and then breaks it.

4. **Preserve Formatting:** Often, you want your text to be exactly in the same style as it is in the HTML document. In these

instances, the preformatted tag <pre> may be used. Any text between the opening <pre> tag and the closing </pre> tag will retain the source document's formatting.

Now I will shortly list as many tags as I can in the brief space accorded. There are thousands of HTML tags. Using these tags you can customize your webpage any way you want:

Table 1.1

- <html> Main container
- <head> The document's header
- <base> Base URI to solve relative URIs
- <title> The document's title
- <link> Relational information for documents
- <style> Presentational attributes
- <meta> Variable for the document
- <article> Distributable content
- <body> The document's body
- <section> Defines a section
- <aside> Content only slightly related
- <nav> Navigational section
- <h1> A level 1 heading, or <h2> A level 2 heading, up to <h6> A level 6 heading
- <header> The header of a section
- <hgroup> Groups consecutive headings
- <footer> The footer of a section
- <address> Author's contact information
- <p> Paragraph
- <pre> Preformatted text block
- <hr> Content separator

- \<blockquote\> Block level quotation
- \<ul\> Unordered list
- \<ol\> Ordered list
- \<li\> List item
- \<dt\> Term in a description list
- \<dl\> Description list
- \<dd\> Description in a description list
- \<figcaption\> Caption for a figure
- \<figure\> Self-contained information
- \<div\> Generic container for blocks of text
- \<main\> Main content of a section
- \<a\> Hyperlink
- \<strong\> Text with strong emphasis
- \<em\> Text with emphasis
- \<small\> Side commment
- \<cite\> Citation or reference
- \<s\> Content no longer accurate or relevant
- \<q\> Inline quotation
- \<abbr\> Abbreviated term
- \<dfn\> Term defined in the surrounding text
- \<ruby\> Ruby annotated text
- \<rp\> Text to be ignored in ruby
- \<rt\> Ruby annotation
- \<data\> Machine-readable information
- \<code\> Computer code
- \<time\> Date and/or time

- `<var>` Instance of a variable
- `<kbd>` Text entered by users
- `<samp>` A program's sample output
- `<sub>` Texto en subíndice
- `<i>` Text offset from the normal prose
- `<sup>` Texto en superíndice
- `<b>` Text offset from its surrounding content
- `<mark>` Marks text in another document
- `<u>` Non-textual annotations
- `<bdi>` Isolates text for bidirectional formatting
- `<span>` Generic container for runs of text
- `<bdo>` Overrides the bidirectional algorithm
- `<ins>` Added text
- `<picture>` Multi-source image
- `<del>` Deleted text
- `<img>` Image
- `<embed>` Inserts external applications
- `<iframe>` Nested browsing context
- `<object>` Inserts external applications
- `<video>` Video
- `<param>` Parameter for an external application
- `<audio>` Audio
- `<track>` Text tracks for videos
- `<source>` Alternative media resource
- `<map>` Client-side image map

- <area> Sector in an image map
- <table> Table
- <colgroup> Group of columns
- <caption> The caption of a table
- <col> Sets attributes for columns
- <thead> The header of the table
- <tbody> The body of the table
- <tfoot> The footer of the table
- <tr> Row
- <th> Header cell
- <td> Regular cell
- <form> Form
- <input> Input control
- <label> Label for a control
- <button> Button
- <datalist> Suggestions for controls
- <select> List of options
- <optgroup> Group of options in a list
- <textarea> Multi-line text input
- <option> An option in list
- <keygen> Key pair generation control
- <progress> A task's completion progress
- <output> The output of a process
- <meter> A measurement
- <legend> The caption of a group of controls
- <fieldset> Group of controls
- <details>   Collapsable

content

- \<menu\> Menu

- \<summary\> A summary for collapsable content

- \<menuitem\> An item in a menu

- \<script\> Embeds scripts

- \<dialog\> Dialog box

- \<noscript\> Alternative content for scripts

- \<canvas\> Container for dynamic bitmap graphics

I hope the above details widened your knowledge of HTML. Now let's move onto CSS, the styling language.

2.2 CSS Fundamentals

Cascading Style Sheets (CSS) is a simple design language designed to make the process of making web pages presentable and easier. As described before, you can use CSS to change the font style, color of the text, background images or colors, paragraph spacing, how columns are sized and laid out, and a variety of other effects. CSS is simple to learn and understand. It gives you a lot of command over how an HTML document looks.

Let's get into the syntax of CSS. The syntax is the basic structure of statements in a program.

Syntax

CSS is made up of style rules that the browser interprets and then applies to the corresponding elements in your document. A style rule consists of three parts:

1. **Selector:** A selector is an HTML tag that specifies where a style will be applied. This could be any tag, such as \<table\> or h1\>

2. **Property:** A property is a type of HTML tag attribute. Simply put, all HTML attributes are transformed into CSS properties. They could be a border, color, or something else.

3. **Value:** Properties are given values. For example, the color property can be either red and so on.

CSS Style Rule Syntax can be written as follows:

- **Selector { property: value }**

As an example: A table border can be defined as follows:

- **Border :1px solid #C00; table**

Table is a selector, border is a property, and the value of that property is given as 1px solid #C00.

Before we move in with the types of selectors, let me put some light on the above value. It must be confusing. We will study CSS Colors and Measurement Units. These two points will help you understand the CSS syntax.

1. CSS Colors

CSS color values are used to specify a color. Usually, these are used to designate a color for an element's foreground (i.e., its text) or context (i.e., its background color). They may also be used to change the color of borders and other decorative features.

Color values can be defined in a variety of formats. The following table has all the possible formats:

- **Hex Code**

  It follows the syntax: **#RRGGBB**

  For Example: p{color:**#FF0000;**}

- **Short Hex Code**

  It follows the syntax: **#RGB**

  For Example: p{color:**#6A7;**}

- **RGB %**

  It follows the syntax: **rgb(rrr%,ggg%,bbb%)**

  For Example: p{color:rgb(50%,50%,50%);}

- **RGB Absolute**

  It follows the syntax: **rgb(rrr,ggg,bbb)**

  For Example: p{color:rgb(0,0,255);}

- **Keyword**

  It follows the syntax: aqua, black, etc.

  For Example: p{color:teal;}

Let me explain the Hex Code in detail, which was used in the earlier example:

Hex Code

A hexadecimal color code is a six-digit representation of a color. The first two digits (RR) represent a red value, the next two represent a green value (GG), and the last two represent a blue value (BB). Any graphics software, such as Jasc Paintshop Pro, Adobe Photoshop, or even Advanced Paint Brush, can be used to generate a hexadecimal value. Each hexadecimal code will be preceded by a pound sign or the hash sign '#.' The following are few examples of how to use Hexadecimal notation.

Table 1.2
- Red #FF0000
- Black #000000
- Green #00FF00
- Yellow #FFFF00
- Dark Blue #0000FF
- Light Blue #00FFFF
- Grey #C0C0C0
- Purple #FF00FF
- White #FFFFFF

This was the basic guide on CSS Colors. Now we will move onto the measurement units.

1. Measurement Units

CSS embraces a broad variety of scales, including absolute units like centimeters, inches, and marks, as well as relative metrics including em and percentages units. These values are needed when defining different measurements in your Style rules, such as border= "1px solid red."

We've listed all of the CSS Measurement Units, along with relevant examples:

- cm

  Defines a centimeter measurement.

- %

  Measurement is defined as a percentage relative to another value, normally an enclosing element.

- em

  A relative calculation of a font's height In em spaces. Since an em unit is equal to the size of a given font if you delegate a font to 12pt, each "em" unit is 12pt. Thus, 2em is 24pt.

- in

  A length in inches is described here.

- ex

  This value determines a measurement in comparison to the x-height of a font. The height of the font's lowercase letter x determines the x-height.

- pc

  Defines a unit of measurement in picas. A pica equals 12 inches, so there are six picas per inch.

- mm

  Defines a millimeter measurement.

These were the measurement units. Now let's continue the selector discussion.

Selector Types

Selectors can be defined in a variety of simple ways to suit your needs. Let me put these selectors in order.

1. **Type Selectors:** This is the same selector that we had earlier. Here's another example of how to color all level 1 headings: **h1 { color: #36CFFF;}**

2. **Descendant Selectors:** Assume you want to apply a style rule to a specific element only when it is contained within another

element. The style rule will only apply to the <em> element when it is inside the <ul> tag, as shown in the following example: **ul em { color: #000000;}**

3. **Universal Selectors:** Rather than choosing elements of a particular type, the universal selector simply matches any element type's name: *** { color: #000000;}**

4. **Class Selectors:** Style rules can be specified based on the class attribute of the components. All elements of that class will be formatted in compliance with the specified law: **.black {color: #000000;}**

This rule makes the content in black for any variable in our document that has the class attribute set to black. You may make it a little more descriptive. **h1.black { color: #000000;}**

This rule only extends to <h1> elements with the class attribute set to black. A given entity may have several class selectors added to it. Consider the following scenario: <p class="center bold"> </p>

This para will be designed by the classes bold and center.

5. **Child Selectors:** There is another kind of selector that is similar to descendants but serves a different purpose. Consider the following scenario: **body > p { color: #000000;}**

If a paragraph is a direct child of the <body> part, this rule will make it black. Other paragraphs placed within other items, such as **<div> or <td>,** will not be affected by this law.

6. **ID Selectors:** Style rules can be specified based on the id attribute of the objects. All elements with that id will be formatted in compliance with the specified law. **#black { color: #000000;}**

This rule makes the content in black for any variable in our document with the id attribute set to black. You may make it a little more descriptive. As an example: **h1#black {color: #000000;}**

Only <h1> elements with the id attribute set to black are rendered in black by this rule.

When used as the basis for descendant selectors, id selectors show their true strength. **#black h2** {color: #000000;}

In this case, all level 2 headings will be shown in black while they are inside tags with the id attribute set to black.

7.   **Attribute Selectors:** Styles can also be applied to HTML elements with unique attributes. The following style rule would align all input elements with a form attribute and a meaning of the text:

input[type="text"]{ color: #000000;}

The benefit of this approach is that the input type= "submit"/> variable is unchanged, and the color is only added to the desired text fields.

The attribute selector is subject to the following rules. The lang attribute defines the natural language of a web page's text.

Table 1.3

- p[lang] - Chooses all paragraph components that have a lang attribute.

- p[lang= "fr"] - Selects all paragraph components with the lang attribute set to "fr."

- p[lang˜= "fr"] - Selects all paragraph components with the lang attribute "fr."

- p[lang|="en"] - Selects all paragraph elements with lang attributes that are exactly "en" or begin with "en-".

---

8.   **Group Selectors:** If you prefer, you can add a theme to multiple selectors. Simply use a comma to distinguish the selectors, as seen in the example below:

Table 1.4

```
h1, h2, h3
{
color: #36C;
letter-spacing: .4em;
font-weight: normal;
text-transform: lowercase;
margin-bottom: 1em;
}
```

This style rule also applies to the h1, h2, and h3 elements. It makes no difference what order the objects are in on the list. The related statements would be added to all the elements in the selector.

9. **Multiple Style Rules:** For a single feature, you may need to specify several style rules. You may use these rules to combine several properties and their corresponding values into a single block, as seen in the example below:

Table 1.5

```
h1
{
color: #36C;
letter-spacing: .4em;
font-weight: normal;
text-transform: lowercase;
margin-bottom: 1em;
}
```

A semicolon separates all of the property and value pairs here (;). You may carry them in a single line or several lines. We keep them on different lines for easy reading.

Now let me help you understand some other basics like font sizing and styling.

Font Size

The font-size property specifies the text dimension.

It is important in web design to be able to monitor the text size. You cannot, though, use font size variations to make headings look like paragraphs or paragraphs look like headings. Always use the appropriate HTML tags, such **as <p> for paragraphs and <h1>-<h6> for headings.**

The font-size value may be either absolute or relative.

1. **Relative Size:** It sets the size in comparison to the elements around it. It allows users to adjust the size of the text in browsers.

2. **Absolute Size:** It resizes the text to a particular scale. In all browsers, it does not enable the user to adjust the text size (not good for accessibility reasons.) When the physical size of the output is known, absolute size is useful.

Let me show that it can be done with em, pixel, or both of them.

1. **Font-Size with Em**

Many programmers use em instead of pixels to allow users to resize text (via the browser menu). 1 em is the same as the new font size. In most browsers, the default text size is 16px. As a result, the default value of 1em is 16px. The following formula can be used to convert pixels to em: pixels/16=em

```
Table 1.6


h1
{
font-size: 2.5em; /* 40px/16=2.5em */
}
h2
{
font-size: 1.875em; /* 30px/16=1.875em */
}
P
{
font-size: 0.875em; /* 14px/16=0.875em */
}
```

2. **Font-Size with Pixels**

When you set the text size in pixels, you have total control over the text size:

Table 1.7

```
h1
{
font-size: 30px;
}
h2
{
font-size: 40px;
}
P
{
font-size: 14px;
}
```

3. **Combining Pixels and Em in Font Size**

Setting a default font-size in percent for the <body> feature is a solution that works in all browsers:

```
Table1.8

Body
{
font-size: 100%;
}
h1
{
font-size: 2.5em;
}
h2
{
font-size: 1.875em;
}
p
{
font-size: 0.875em;
}
```

Do you know something about viewport width? Let me tell you.

Responsive Font Size

The text size can be changed using a vw tool, which stands for "viewport width." As a result, the text size will adjust to match the size of the browser window.

```
Table 1.9
<h1 style="font-size:10vw">Hello World</h1>
```

Just like the sizing of the fonts, positioning, styling is also an important feature. Let me tell you a few things about it.

1. **Font Styling:** Italic text is usually defined using the font-style property. There are three values for this property:

- Italic - The text is italicized.

- Normal - The text appears normally.

- Oblique -The text is "leaning" in an oblique way (oblique is very similar to italic.)

```
Table 1.10
p.normal {font-style: normal;}
p.italic {font-style: italic;}
p.oblique {font-style: oblique;}
```

2. **Font Variant:** The font-variant property determines whether text can be written in small caps or not.

All lowercase letters in a small-caps font are translated to uppercase letters. The transformed uppercase letters, on the other hand, appear in a smaller font size than the initial uppercase letters in the text.

Table 1.11

p.normal {font-variant: normal;}

p.small {font-variant: small-caps;}

Font Weight: The font-weight property determines a font's weight:

Table 1.12

p.normal {font-weight: normal;}

p.thick {font-weight: bold;}

Let me show you a model which will help you in positioning and layout of content.

1. **CSS Box Model:** When discussing design and layout in CSS, the expression "box model" is used.

    The CSS box model consists of a box that wraps around any HTML feature. It is made up of the following elements: margins, padding, borders, and the actual text.

    Explanation of the various parts:

    ·   Padding - Adds space around the content. The padding is see-through.

    ·   Content - The box's content, which contains text and pictures.

    ·   Margin - Excludes a portion of the area beyond the boundary. The margin is transparent.

    ·   Boundary - A boundary is a line that circles the padding and text.

    The box model helps one to identify space between elements and add a boundary around them.

For example:

```
Table 1.13

div {
width: 300px;
border: 15px solid green;
padding: 50px;
margin: 20px;
}
```

To correctly set the height and width of an element in all browsers, you must understand how the box model operates. When you use CSS to set the width and height properties of an element, you are simply setting the width and height of the content field. You must also account for borders, padding, and margins when calculating the maximum size of an element.

This <div> element will have a whole width of 350px:

Table 1.14

```
div {
padding: 10px;
width: 320px;
margin: 0;
border: 5px solid gray;
}
```

Let me explain:

Table 1.15

320px (width)

+ 20px (left + right padding)

+ 10px (left + right border)

+ 0px (left + right margin)

= 350px

This is the formula to calculate the height and width of an element:

· Total element height = top padding + height + bottom padding + bottom border + top border + bottom margin + top margin

- Total element width = left padding + width + right padding + right border + left border + right margin +left margin

These were some CSS basics that were necessary to start your coding journey. I think with all this knowledge, you have learned enough about HTML and CSS to finally create your own webpage. Let's start coding!

2.3 Creating a Basic Webpage

Pick your favorite hobby. Now I will help you create a website on your favorite hobby with text and images. Let's get straight into it. There are many approaches to developing and managing website programs. Any variance exists depending on the particular instruments you have and the organization's priorities. When developing a website, it is not unusual for the project layout to evolve over time as the project becomes more complex. The key is to maintain a semblance of structure, and there are some common tactics that can help. Major tasks often necessitate a higher level of care and commitment in order for a large number of individuals to keep track of everything. I will discuss everything step by step:

1. **Create a Folder**

Open Visual Studio Code software. The Welcome page appears when you open Visual Studio Code. You will see that you can make a new file or open a folder. You can also do this by selecting File > New File.

If the Welcome window is not available, go to Support > Welcome to pull it up. Alternatively, use the shortcut Shift+Command+P or View > Command Palette. Enter >Help: Welcome to the search area.

Select Open folder from the Welcome page's Start section, or go to Folder > Open.

When you open a folder, the operating system gives you the option to make a New Folder. Pick New Folder and navigate to the directory where you want to create the new folder. Simply name the folder basic-website.

2. Create Files

Choose File > New File.

Press Command+S (macOS) or Control+S (Windows) to save the file. "Index.html" should be the name of the file.

Repeat the previous steps to render two more files, app.js and main.css. When you are finished, your project folder will include the following files, which form your website:

- index.html
- app.js
- main.css

Do not worry about the app.js file for now. It is for JavaScript, which we will cover in the next chapter. In the Explorer window, you can see the three files that make up the website under the folder name.

You may build a website entirely from text or HTML files. For content and page layout, you are using an HTML format. A CSS file is used to style and present content. The JavaScript file is used for interactivity and behaviors.

Creating three folders allows us to remain balanced. It exemplifies radical enhancement. CSS and HTML will still work if JavaScript is not allowed or supported. However, if CSS does not function, the HTML content will be shown.

3. Install Packages or Extensions

The extensions marketplace allows you to expand the capabilities of Visual Studio Code. Keep in mind that these are community-created tools. There are most often multiple solutions for the same type of feature. You can add extensions one at a time in your editor, or you can use the command line to install several extensions at once.

What you need right now for web creation is an open-in-browser. Instead of copying and pasting the file URL into your window, this extension allows you to easily access the website in your regular browser.

To install this extension, follow these steps:

- On the Activity Bar, press the Extensions button (left pane).

- Enter "open in" into the search bar, then choose ``open in browser'', published by TechER, and press install. The extension is now installed.

- Return to the Explorer browser.

You currently have an empty HTML file. Let's put the coding in. The aim is to use hypertext markup language to define the web page that should be displayed by the browser.

4. Writing HTML Code

Visual Studio Code includes basic HTML programming support out of the box. Syntax highlighting, IntelliSense smart completions, and flexible formatting are all available.

- Open index.html in Visual Studio Code by clicking the index.html file. Select the index.html tab, type html:5, and click Enter. The HTML5 template code is appended to the file.

- Edit the code to look like this, and then save the file by pressing Command+S (macOS) or Control+S (Windows)

```
Table 1.16
<!DOCTYPE html>
<html lang="en">
<head>
<meta charset="UTF-8">
<title> My First Webpage </title>
</head>
<body>
</body>
</html>
```

HTML has several versions. HTML5 coding is indicated by the text type <!DOCTYPE html>.

Although we would not again go into depth about the context of each HTML feature, we will illustrate a few key points. As mentioned before, the meta tag shows metadata detail that the user would not normally see until they open the source code in their browser. Meta elements, also known as tags, contain descriptive information about a website. They assist search engines, for example, in showing results.

The UTF-8-character set (charset) may seem meaningless, but it is critical for determining how computers view characters. In the absence of a charset, stability can be jeopardized. There is a lot of history and technological knowledge that goes into charset.

Coding the Head

The title of a website, which appears at the top of a browser window, is important in many respects. For example, search engines use and display the title. Let's give it a word. You can write the name of your hobby.

An important thing to remember is that the ellipsis (...) means that the previously declared code arrives before or after this point. As background, there should be enough code given to allow any required adjustments or improvements to your job.

Table 1.17

...

\<head>

\<meta charset="utf-8">

\<title> My First Webpage \</title>

...

You could write the CSS code directly in the website's head to style the HTML elements on the document, which is known as internal CSS. It is, however, best practice to keep HTML layout and CSS styling apart. Getting a different CSS tab is referred to as external CSS. When code is clear and compartmentalized, it is easier to understand. To service several web pages, you can use one or more external style sheets. Rather than duplicating CSS on each HTML tab, you can make changes once and have them broadcast on all dependent sites. Let's add a link to an external style sheet.

- Add a blank line after the title> element in Visual Studio Code, enter link css, and then hit "Enter."

- Change the href from style.css to main.css and save the file with Command+S (Mac) (macOS) or Control+S (Windows.)

You should have this product.

```
Table 1.18


...

<head>

<meta charset="utf-8">


<title> My First Webpage </title>

<link rel="stylesheet" href="main.css">

</head>

...
```

5. Coding the Body

Let's get started on the body part right away. Develop a heading <h1>, a paragraph <p>, and a list item <li>. Edit the code, or copy and paste it, so that it looks like this.

Table 1.19

```html
<!DOCTYPE html>
<html lang="en" dir="ltr">
<head>
<meta charset="utf-8">

<title> My First Webpage </title>
<link rel="stylesheet" href="main.css">
</head>
<body>

<h1>Task List</h1>
<p id="msg">Current tasks:</p>
<ul>
<li class="list">Add visual styles</li>
<li class="list">Add light and dark themes</li>

<li>Enable switching the theme</li>
</ul>
</body>
</html>
```

An ID attribute (as used in the <p>) can be used to style a single element, while the class attribute (as used in the <li>) can be used to style all elements of the same class.

Each <li> variable in the list is grouped into an unordered list <ul>.

6. Coding for Images

Images can enhance the look and presentation of a website. It will look like this in coding:

<img src="img_girl.jpg" alt="Girl in a jacket">

Let me help you with the details:

To insert an image in a web-page, use the HTML <img> tag.

Images are connected to websites rather than being embedded into them. The img> tag provides a space holder for the referenced file.

The img> tag is empty; it only includes attributes and lacks a closing tag.

Two attributes are necessary for the <img> tag:

Table 1.20

alt - Specifies an alternative text for the image

src - Specifies the direction to the image

<img src="url" alt="alternatetext">

The height and width of an image may be defined using the style attribute like this:

Table 1.21

<img src="img_girl.jpg" alt="Girl in a jacket" width="500" height="600">

7. Browser Check

You will see a local overview of your website by opening the HTML file in a tab. Instead of a website address beginning with https://, your browser leads you to a local file route. For e.g., the path could resemble the following: index.html can be found at file:/Users/username/Desktop/public/index.html.

To preview index.html in Visual Studio Code, right-click it and select "Open in Default Window", or use the shortcut Alt+B.

The page will open in your default tab. **Developer Tools Check**

Using the developer software in your browser, you can inspect a webpage. Let's give it a shot.

- Open Developer Tools.

- In Edge, click the Developer Tools keyboard shortcut, F12 (FN+F12). Alternatively, click Alt+X and pick Developer Tools to display Configurations and more.

- In Chrome, click the Developer Tools keyboard shortcut, Option+Command+I. (F12 is also an option.)

- Choose the Elements tab.

- Roll your mouse over the HTML elements to pick them.

- Enable the drop down triangles.

In developer tools, the Elements tab displays the document object model (DOM) as it is created in the browser. When debugging, it is often appropriate to observe how the browser interprets the source code.

Voila, this is your basic HTML document. Do you like our website so far? It is a bit bland, right? Are you ready to make it pretty? Then let's proceed with CSS.

CSS (Cascading Style Sheets) allows you to decide how your page should look. The basic concept is to target HTML code and then specify the style. You may, for example, pick a box and add rounded corners or a gradient backdrop to it. While you specify the destination address in HTML, CSS is responsible for deciding how hyperlinks look and behave when you communicate with them. CSS3 also allows for complex animation effects.

8. External CSS

Just now, you had linked from HTML to an external CSS file.

Table 1.22

...

```
<head>
<meta charset="utf-8">
<title>Task Timeline</title>
<link rel="stylesheet" href="main.css">
...
```

External CSS has the advantage of allowing several HTML pages to connect to the same CSS file. If you make a CSS adjustment, the style will be updated for each page. Separation of concerns refers to the process of designating an HTML file for page layout, a CSS file for decoration, and a JavaScript file for contact or activities.

As previously said, you can also write CSS directly in HTML, which is known as internal CSS. Even for a simple website, there are so many CSS guidelines that the HTML page easily gets cluttered. With several pages, the same CSS will often be replicated and difficult to handle.

9. Key CSS Rules

Assume you have an old-fashioned key and a long hallway with a set of doors. You pick a door and then use the key to open it. You can decorate a room however you like until you have keys to it. You may paint the walls yellow or add a hardwood floor. You chose space and set the rules for how it should look. The same style can be applied to different spaces, much like CSS.

Open the main.css file in Visual Studio Code and type the following.

```
Table 1.23
body {
font-family: monospace;
}
ul {
font-family: helvetica;
}
```

CSS guidelines can be used to format HTML. The unordered list element ul is a selector that selects the <ul> HTML element to which styles are added. The declaration is font-family: Helvetica, and it defines the type. The name of the property is font-family. The value is Helvetica. A key-value pair is formed by the property and the value.

What you are selecting is an established HTML entity (<body> and <ul>) that you previously identified. You should define your own custom names for components, as you will see next.

10. CSS Selectors

Styles can be added to custom attribute names in your HTML using ID and class selectors. A class can style several objects, while an ID can only style one.

- After the ul selector you previously inserted, paste the following code into your CSS file.

Table 1.24

```
li {
list-style: circle;
}
.list {
list-style: square;
}
#msg {
font-family: monospace;
}
```

The two preceding custom attributes are. list and #msg. The class selector list begins with a period, while the ID selector begins with a pound sign. The names can be anything you want as long as they complement what you have specified in the HTML.

- Save your work now.

11. Browser Check

To view the preview in Visual Studio Code, right-click index.html. Then choose "Open In Default Browser."

It is fascinating to see how styles flow from body to h1. Since we did not describe anything for h1, it gets its styling from the body. However, since you specified a style for it, this takes priority over the body tag.

12. Applying a Light Theme

Then, for your website, add support for a color theme. Begin by establishing a light-colored color scheme. Using hex color codes for the light theme. Choose (#000000, black) for the font color and (#00FF00, a green hue) for the background color.

- Insert the following code at the end of your CSS file.

Table 1.25
```
.light-theme {
color: #000000;
background: #00FF00;
}
```

- Update the <body> element in your HTML file with the class name light-theme so that the class selector for the light theme can apply the styles correctly.

Table 1.26
```
<body class="light-theme">
```

13. Browser Check

To view the preview in Visual Studio Code, right-click index.html. Then choose "Open In Default Browser." The page will open in your default tab. Take note of the appearance of the light theme with a green backdrop.

14. Observe Applied CSS

- Open Developer Tools.

  o In Edge, click the Developer Tools keyboard shortcut, F12 (FN+F12). Alternatively, click Alt+X and pick Developer Tools to display Configurations and more.

  o In Chrome, click the Developer Tools keyboard shortcut, Option+Command+I. (F12 is also an option.)

  · Choose the Styles tab.

  · Choose the Elements tab.

  · Roll your mouse over the HTML elements to pick them.

  · Choose the <body> element. Take note of the light theme used.

  · Enable the transparency triangles.

  · Choose a <li> element. Take note of the custom type font-family: Helvetica, which overrides the body> element's style.

  ·

15. Applying a Dark Theme

You are now going to set up the infrastructure for the dark theme in preparation for the next chapter, in which you allow theme swapping on the web page.

To allow support for a dark theme, follow these steps:

- In your CSS code, add some constants to the page base.

```
Table 1.27
:root {
–green: #00FF00;
–white: #ffffff;
–black: #000000;
```

The :root selector represents the HTML page's <html> feature. The best practice for this form of job is to specify a collection of global CSS variables in the :root element. In this section, you specify three color variables that are linked to the page base.

- Add the dark-theme selector at the end of the CSS file and change the light-theme selector.

Table 1.28

```
.light-theme {
–bg: var(–green);
–fontColor: var(–black);


}

.dark-theme {
–bg: var(–black);
–fontColor: var(–green);
}
```

In the preceding code, you specified two new variables, bg, and fontColor, to determine the background and font colors, respectively. To define variables to be used as property values, use the var keyword. You previously set the values in your :root selector.

- Next, in your CSS format, replace the existing body selector with the following after the :root selector.

Table 1.29

```css
* {
color: var(--fontColor);
font-family: helvetica;
}


body {
background: var(--bg);
}
```

The * selector is a global selector that affects all page components (except where a more specified element selector overrides it). It is used to set the default color property for all page elements in this case. You specify the variables specified in the dark and light theme selectors for the color and background properties.

- Remove the #msg selector from your CSS so that we can use the same font for all components.

- To see the dark theme, change the default theme in the <body> element to a dark theme (dark-theme). Then open the page in the browser.

- To return the default theme to light, edit the body> portion.

In the following chapter, you can use JavaScript to enable interactivity and enable theme switching.

Chapter 3: Making your Webpage Interactive through JavaScript

In the previous chapter, you developed a basic structure of your website and learned how you could add some styling to it. Now, it is time to add functionality to your website. JavaScript is your best friend to do just that. Before we proceed with it, let's understand the essentials and working of JavaScript.

3.1 JavaScript Fundamentals

JavaScript is the most common open-source, client-side scripting language, and it is supported by all browsers. JavaScript is mostly used to improve the engagement of a website with its visitors by making it more colorful and engaging. It is also used in the development of gaming and smartphone apps.

Almost every newcomer to web development begins with the same topic: HTML. HTML does not have much interactivity of its own, but most pages still look sharp and interactive. JavaScript helps achieve that. JavaScript is used to incorporate interactive features to websites such as slideshows, pop-ups, animated graphics, forms, and other personalized content.

JavaScript (abbreviated JS) is a dynamic, lightweight scripting language that was created to support prototype-based programming. It is mostly used for front-end development, but it does have a Node.js module for server-side scripting. We talked about Node.js earlier. Node.js is a tool for quickly creating easy and flexible network apps. It is based on Chrome's JavaScript runtime. Node.js server is praised by developers for its reliability and ability to render easily on both browsers and servers. As a result, its prominence is rapidly increasing.

Before we get into the important features of JavaScript, let's study the basic JavaScript Syntax.

JavaScript Syntax

JavaScript can be used to create web pages by inserting JavaScript statements between the <script>... </script> HTML tags. You can put the <script> tags containing your JavaScript anywhere on your web page. It is usually best to keep it within the <head> tags. The <script> tag instructs the browser to begin reading all text between these tags as a script. The following is a basic syntax for your JavaScript:

Table 2.1

<script ...>
JavaScript code
</script>

The script tag needs two key attributes:

- **Language:** This variable describes the scripting language that is being used. Its value is usually JavaScript. However, modern iterations of HTML (and its descendant, XHTML) have phased out the use of this attribute.

- **Type:** It is now proposed that this attribute is set to "text/JavaScript" to indicate the scripting language in use.

As a result, the JavaScript syntax would look like this.

Table 2.2

```
<script language="javascript" type="text/javascript">
JavaScript code
</script>
```

Let's have an example to help you understand better:

Let's try printing "Hello Friends" as an example. We inserted an optional HTML statement around our JavaScript file. This is done to secure our JavaScript from browsers that do not support JavaScript. The statement concludes with a "/—>." Since "//" in JavaScript represents a comment, we include it here to prevent a browser from reading the ending of the HTML comment as a piece of JavaScript text. Then we have to call a function document.write, which inserts a string into our HTML document.

This feature can be used to write HTML, text, or both at the same time. Have a look at the code below.

Table 2.3

```
<html>
<body>
<script                    language="javascript"
type="text/javascript">
<!–
 document.write ("Hello Friends!")
//–>
</script>
</body>
</html>
```

You should understand a few concepts about syntax. Let me list them for you:

1. **Semicolons:** Simple statements in JavaScript, like those in C, Java, and C++ are usually accompanied by a semicolon character. JavaScript, on the other hand, helps you to omit this semicolon if each of the sentences is on a different side. The following code, for example, may be written without semicolons.

Table 2.4

```
<script language="javascript" type="text/javascript">
<!--
 var1 = 10
 var2 = 20
//-->
</script>
```

However, semicolons must be used when formatted in a single line, as seen below:

Table 2.5

```
<script language="javascript" type="text/javascript">
<!--
var1 = 10; var2 = 20;
//-->
</script>
```

If you do not understand these codes completely, do not worry. I yet have to explain all the terms that you will need to know in JavaScript.

2.   **Line Breaks and Whitespace:** JavaScript ignores tabs, spaces, and newlines in JavaScript programs. You can freely use tabs, spaces, and newlines in your software, and you can format and indent your programs in a tidy and clear fashion that makes the code easily understandable.

3.   **Comments:** JavaScript comments can be used to clarify and improve the readability of JavaScript code. When checking alternative code, JavaScript comments can also be used to avoid execution. JavaScript accepts comments written in both C and C++ syntax. So:

·   Any content between a / and the end of a line is considered a comment by JavaScript and is ignored.

·   Any text between the characters /* and */ is considered to be a comment. This may stretch many lines.

·   JavaScript also understands the HTML comment opening sequence <!—. This is treated as a single-line comment by JavaScript, much like the / comment.

·   Since JavaScript does not know the HTML comment closing sequence -->, it should be written as //—>

This will help you:

Table 2.6

```
<script language="javascript" type="text/javascript">
<!–
// It is a comment. It is like the comments in C++
/*
* It is a multi-line comment in JavaScript
* This is much like the comments in C Programming
*/
//–>
</script>
```

4. **Case Sensitivity:** JavaScript is a case-sensitive programming language. This implies that all language variables, keywords, function names, and other identifiers must be typed with consistent letter capitalization.

> As a consequence, in JavaScript, the identifiers TIME and Time would have separate meanings.

Before we dig deep into the JavaScript important features, you should know about a few things about JavaScript placement:

Placement

The ability to use JavaScript code anywhere in an HTML document is supported. However, the most common methods for using JavaScript in an HTML file are as follows:

- Script in <body>...</body> section: If you need a script to run as the page loads and create content for the page, put it in the <body> section of the text. In this case, you will not have any JavaScript-defined functions.

- Script in <head>...</head> section: If you want a script to run on a certain event, such as when a user clicks somewhere, put it in the head.

- Script in an external file and then include in <head>...</head> section: You are not bound to maintain similar code in different HTML files.

- The script tag allows you to store JavaScript in an external file and then use it in your HTML files.

- Script in <body>...</body> and <head>...</head> sections: You can place the JavaScript code in both the <head> and <body> parts.

It is time to study JavaScript features:

1. Variables

Variables are used in JavaScript, as they are in many other programming languages. Variables can be interpreted as labeled containers. You should put data in these containers and only refer to it by calling the container.

A variable is required to be declared prior to being used in a JavaScript application. Variables are declared through the var keyword, as seen below:

```
Table 2.7

<script type="text/javascript">
<!–
var money;
var name;
//–>
</script>
```

You may also use the very same keyword of var to declare different variables, as seen below:

```
Table 2.8

<script type="text/javascript">
<!–
var money, name;
//–>
</script>
```

Variable initialization is the method of saving a value inside a variable. Variable initialization may be done at the variable development time or at some other time when the variable is needed.

For example, you might construct a variable called money and later add the value 2010.10 to it. You may add a value to another variable during initialization, as seen below.

```
Table 2.9


<script type="text/javascript">
<!–
var name = "Ali";
var money;
money = 2010.10;
//–>
</script
```

Use the var keyword only once for initialization or declaration of any variable name in a script. You are not allowed to declare the same variable more than once. JavaScript is an untyped programming language. This means that a JavaScript variable can have any data type as a value. Unlike certain other languages, JavaScript does not require you to define the type of value the variable would contain during variable declaration. The value type of a variable will alter during program execution, and JavaScript handles it automatically.

What is the scope of these variables?

A variable's scope is the area of your software where it is specified. Variables in JavaScript have only two scopes.

- A local variable is only observable inside the function in which it is described. The parameters of a function are still local to that function.

- Global variables have global scope, which means that they can be specified anywhere in your JavaScript code.

A local variable with the same name takes priority over a global variable with the same name inside the body of a function. When you declare a function parameter or local variable of the same name as a global variable, you have essentially hidden the global variable.

Variable Rules

Bear the following rules in mind when naming variables in JavaScript.

- Variable names in JavaScript should not begin with a number (0-9). They must start with an underscore character or letter. 123test, for example, is an invalid variable name, but _123test is a legitimate one.

- Variable names in JavaScript are case-sensitive. Name and name, for example, are two separate variables.

- As a variable name, you cannot use any of the JavaScript reserved keywords. They cannot be used as JavaScript functions, variables, loop labels, methods, or any object names.

·This is a list of these keywords:

- Boolean
- abstract
- break
- case
- byte
- catch

- class
- char
- const
- debugger
- continue
- default
- do
- delete
- double
- enum
- else
- export
- false
- extends
- final
- float
- finally
- for
- goto
- implements
- if
- import
- instanceof
- int
- in
- long
- interface

- native
- null
- new
- package
- protected
- private
- public
- short
- return
- static
- switch
- super
- synchronized
- throw
- this
- throws
- true
- transient
- try
- var
- typeof
- void
- while
- volatile
- with

Operators are another significant feature:

2. Operators

Let us consider a simple expression. The sum of 5 and 4 is 9. The numbers 4 and 5 are referred to as operands, and the symbol '+' is referred to as the operator. The following operators are supported by JavaScript:

- **Comparison Operators:** The JavaScript programming language contains operators that compare two operands and return a Boolean value of false or true. Do you remember that a JavaScript Boolean has two possible values: true or false?

  Ø Compares the equality of two operands with type. (===)

  Ø Compares the equality of two operands without taking type into account. (==)

  Ø Compares the inconsistency of two operands. (!=)

  Ø Determines if the left operand is smaller than the right operand. If yes, returns true; otherwise, returns false. (<)

  Ø Determines if the left-side value is higher than the right-side value. If yes, returns true; otherwise, returns false. (>)

  Ø Determines whether the left operand is equal or less than the right operand. If yes, returns true; otherwise, returns false. (<=)

  Ø = Determines whether the left operand is greater than or equal to the right operand. If yes, returns true; otherwise, returns false. (>=)

Let me help you understand more:

Table 2.10

```
var a = 5, b = 10, c = "5";
var x = a;

a === c; // returns false

a == c; // returns true

a == x; // returns true

a > b; // returns false

a != b; // returns true

a < b; // returns true

a <= b; // returns true

a >= b; // returns false

a <= c; // returns true
a >= c; // returns true
```

- **Arithmetic operators:** These operators are used to execute operations between numerical operands.

Ø - Takes the right operand and subtracts it from the left operand.

Ø + Combines two numeric operands.

Ø * Add two numeric operands together.

Ø % Modulus operator. The remainder of the two operands is returned.

Ø / Divide the left operand from the right operand.

Ø -- Decrement Operator. Reduce the meaning by one.

Ø ++ Increment operator. Increase the value of the operand by one.

This is how you use these operators:

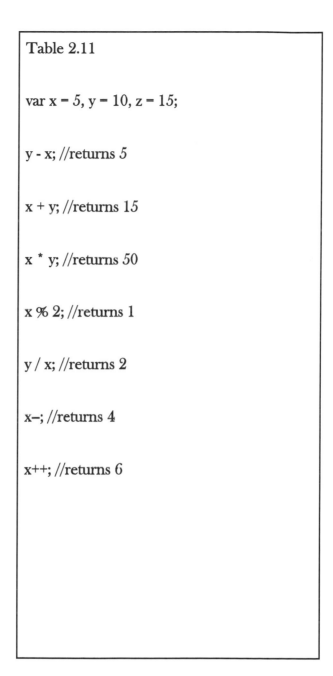

Table 2.11

var x = 5, y = 10, z = 15;

y - x; //returns 5

x + y; //returns 15

x * y; //returns 50

x % 2; //returns 1

y / x; //returns 2

x–; //returns 4

x++; //returns 6

· **Logical Operators:** These are used to integrate two or more conditions:

Ø The OR operator is defined by ||. It determines whether one of the two operands is non-zero (false, 0, null, undefined, or "" is considered zero).

Ø The AND operator is represented by &&. It determines if two operands are non-zero (false, 0, null, unknown, or ""are called zero) and returns 1 if yes, otherwise 0.

Ø The NOT operator is represented by ! It flips the operand's boolean result (or condition)

For example,

Table 2.12

var a = 5, b = 10;

(a > b) || (a == b); // returns false

(a != b) && (a < b); // returns true

(a < b) || (a == b); // returns true

!(a > b); // returns true

!(a < b); // returns false

·   **Ternary operator (:?):** It is a special operator in JavaScript that assigns a value to a variable depending on some condition. This is a shortened version of the if-else condition.

The syntax goes as <condition>? <value1> : <value2>;

The ternary operator begins with a conditional expression and is followed by the ? operator. If the condition is valid, the second element (after the ? and before the : operator) will be executed. If the procedure fails, the third element (after :) will be executed.

For example,

Table 2.13

var a = 10, b = 5;

var d = a > b? b : a; // value of d would be 5
var c = a > b? a : b; // value of c would be 10

·   **Assignment Operators:** JavaScript has assignment operators that allow you to assign values to variables with fewer keystrokes. Here they are:

Ø += Adds the values of the left and right operands and assigns the sum to the left operand.

Ø = Assigns the right operand value to the left operand.

Ø -= Deducts the value of the right operand from the value of the left operand and adds the result to the left operand.

Ø /= Divide the value of the left operand by the value of the right operand and assign the result to the left operand.

Ø *= Multiplies the right and left operands and assigns the result to the left operand.

Ø % = Takes the modulus of the left operand, divides it by the modulus of the right operand, and allocates the resultant modulus to the left operand.

Have a look at this:

Table 2.14
var x = 5, y = 10, z = 15;
x += 1; //x would be 6
x = y; //x would be 10
x -= 1; //x would be 4
x /= 5; //x would be 1
x *= 5; //x would be 25
x %= 2; //x would be 1

Now moving onto functions:

3. Function

A function in JavaScript is a code piece that is programmed to execute a specific purpose. When "something" triggers a JavaScript method, it is executed. Like:

- If a specific incident happens (when a user clicks a button)
- Automatically (self-invoked)

- When it is invoked from JavaScript code

For instance,

```
Table 2.15
function myFunction(p2, p1) {


return p2 * p1; // The function "returns" the product of p2
and p1
}
```

Benefits of Functions

You have to define the code once. Then you can reuse it many times. The same code can be run several times with different arguments to achieve different results. For example, let's convert Fahrenheit to Celsius:

```
Table 2.16
function toCelsius(fahrenheit) {


return (5/9) * (fahrenheit-32);
}
document.getElementById("demo").innerHTML          =
toCelsius(77);
```

Keep these things in mind:

- The keyword function, preceded by a name, then by parentheses, is used to describe a JavaScript function.

- Digits, letters, dollar signs, and underscores will also be found in feature names (with the same rules like that of variables).

- Parameter names divided by commas can be used in the parentheses:

- (parameter 1, parameter 2, etc.)

- The function's code to be carried out is enclosed in curly brackets: {} Look here:

Table 2.17

function name(parameter3, parameter2, parameter1 {

  // code to be carried out

}

- In the function description, function parameters are specified within parentheses ().

- The values passed to the function as it is referred to as function arguments.

- The parameters (arguments) are viewed like local variables within the function.

Here's how function return happens:

Function Return

The function will stop running when it enters a return statement in JavaScript. JavaScript will "return" to run the code that preceded the invoking statement, if the function is called from a statement. Functions also generate a return value. The return value is then "returned" to the "caller" as follows:

Table 2.18

var x = myFunction(4, 3); // Function is invoked, "return" value will end up in x

function myFunction(b, a) {

return b * a; // Function "returns" the product of a and b
}

AS a result, X is equal to 12.

It is important to understand the following:

Function without ()

In the first example, toCelsius denotes the function object. Here, toCelsius() denotes the function output. When you call a function without (), the function object is returned in place of the function result.

Do you want to know how functions are used as variable values?

Variable Values and Functions

Functions, including variables, can be found in all kinds of assignments, formulas, and calculations.

You can utilize the function as a variable value directly, like this:

Table 2.19

var text = "The 'temperature' is " + toCelsius(77) + " Celsius";

Lastly, I want to tell you about local variables.

Local Variables

When variables are declared within a function of JavaScript, they become LOCAL to the function. Only from inside the function can local variables be accessed. For example,

---

Table 2.20

// code here can NOT use carName

function myFunction() {
  var carName = "Volvo";
  // code here CAN use carName
}

// code here can NOT use carName

Variables of the very same name can be found in various functions because local variables are only known within their functions. When a function begins, local variables are generated. They are removed when the function ends.

I hope you have now learned functions in detail, we will move to the next feature, i.e., strings.

4. Strings

Strings in JavaScript are used to store and manipulate code. A JavaScript string consists of zero or more characters enclosed in quotation marks. For example,

Table 2.21

```
var x = "John Doe";
```

You may make use of double or single quotation marks. You can use quotes inside a string as long as they do not match the quotes around it:

Use the length property which is built-in to determine the length of a string:

Table 2.22

```
var txt = "AVCDCJCDBJVKBXYZ";
var sln = txt.length;
```

While learning about strings, you should not miss the following:

Escape character

Since strings must be written inside quotations, JavaScript may interpret this string incorrectly:

The string will be cut to read "We are the so-called." The backslash escape character can be used to prevent this problem. The escape character backslash () converts unique characters into string characters:

Code	Result	Description
\'	'	Single quote
\"	"	Double quote
\\	\	Backslash

In JavaScript, six more escape sequences are valid. Here are these codes with results:

Table 2.24

　\f Form Feed

　\b Backspace

　\n New Line

　\t Horizontal Tabulator

　\r Carriage Return

　\v Vertical Tabulator

Programmers often choose to avoid code lines longer than 80 characters in order to improve readability. If a JavaScript sentence cannot fit in a single line, it is better to split it after an operator.

Table 2.25

document.getElementById("demo").innerHTML = "Hello Dolly!";

A single backslash can also be used to separate code lines within a text string. String extension is a better way to split up a string. A backslash cannot be used to split up a code line.

Let's move forward.

5. Array

It has been established that a variable may only contain one value, so if var i = 1/0, we can only add one value (literal) to i. You are not allowed to give variable i several literal values. JavaScript consists of an array to solve this query.

An array is a kind of variable that can hold several values with the help of special syntax. Each value is assigned a numeric index beginning with 0. I have put a table below that shows how arrays hold values.

12	"Hello"	"Fried"	34	90	2.3	2	3	87
0	1	2	3	4	5	6	7	8

There are two ways to initialize and describe an array in JavaScript: Array constructor syntax and array literals.

- **Array Constructor:** We can use the new keyword to initialize an array by using the syntax of Array constructor.

  The Array constructor comes in three kinds.

  Table 2.26

  Ø var arrayName = new Array(Parenthesis);

  Ø var arrayName = new Array(ElementN);

  Ø var arrayName = new Array(Length of Numbers);

As seen in the preceding syntax, an array, like an entity, may be initialized with the new keyword.

Please keep in mind that arrays are allowed to have only numeric index (key). The index value cannot be a string or some other data type.

- **Array Literal:** The syntax for array literals is straightforward. It accepts a list of values divided by commas and surrounded by square brackets:

  var <array-name> = [ElementN];

  The elements (values) of an array can be obtained using index (key). To access the element at a specific index, identify an index in square brackets with the array name. Please bear in mind that in JavaScript, the array index begins at 0.

  Arrays have a "length" property that returns the element numbers in the series. Using the length attribute, use a for loop to obtain all the array elements.

That was all about JavaScript. Now we will continue where we left in the previous chapter. It is time for you to make your website interactive.

3.2 Adding Functionality to Webpage

Before we move forward, I want to make your concepts clear on how HTML, CSS, and JavaScript work together. To simplify it, I will refer to these three web languages as separate parts of the human body. Consider the body as a command center, the accessories that are placed on the body to reflect the personal style and the behaviors that the body is capable of as a means of animating ourselves. For the purpose of this discussion, HTML will be regarded as the actual body, CSS will be referred to as the body's accessories, and JavaScript will be referred to as the body's ability to speak or move. Many of these 'bodily dimensions' must work together to create a robust, visually pleasing, and engaging website.

Let's revise. JavaScript (also known as ECMAScript) is a programming language that allows you to bring interactivity to your website. When you tap a button, JavaScript is the code that determines what will happen, such as opening a pop-up window. Using JavaScript, you can remove or add content in a webpage, such as text, without having to reload it. You can use the browser as a web developer to test and receive feedback on your scripts.

Let's give your website a voice. Do you remember we prepared codes for two themes for your website? Let's continue from there.

1. Link JavaScript

JavaScript, like CSS, may be added directly to the HTML tab, but it is preferable not to. For e.g., you might add <script>alert('Hello Friend')</script> anywhere in the body to generate a pop-up alert. We may use the script tag <script> to connect to an external JavaScript file.

- Enter script: src into Visual Studio Code and press Enter.

- Change the script variable to look like this. Place it right after the list.

Table 2.27

```
<ul>
  <li class="list">Add visual styles</li>
  <li class="list">Add light and dark themes</li>
  <li>Enable switching the theme</li>
</ul>
<script src="app.js"></script>
```

The script factor may be put anywhere in the <body> or <head>. Putting <Script> at the ending of the <body> line, on the other hand, allows all of the page material to be shown on the screen before loading the script.

2. Add Fault Tolerance

Follow these steps:

- Add the <noscript> attribute to the HTML file, which can be used to view a message if JavaScript is disabled.

Table 2.28

<script src="app.js"></script>

<noscript>You are required to enable JavaScript to see the full site.</noscript>

The use of the <noscript> element is an example of graceful degradation or fault tolerance. When a function is not supported or usable, we can detect and prepare for it.

- Use the shortcut Command+S (macOS) or Control+S (Windows) to save the updates (macOS).

3. Set Strict Mode

As you get started with JavaScript, the initial focus is often working with numbers, math, text manipulation, dates, and storing information. Sometimes JavaScript has assumptions about the type of data you enter - assignment, math, or logical equality can give you unexpected results. JavaScript tries to be friendly, make your code work, and provide you with a solution, even if the result should be an error. To combat these shortcomings, you can activate the strict mode, which reduces silent errors, improves performance, provides more warnings and fewer unsafe features.

In Visual Studio Code, open the app.js file, and enter the following:

4. Add a Button

You must have a method for the user to choose between the light and dark themes on your website. In this case, you use a button feature to accomplish this.

- Insert a <button> feature into your HTML page. Insert the button at the ending of the list inside a <div> variable.

Table 2.29

```
<ul>
  <li class="list">Add visual styles</li>
  <li class="list">Add light and dark themes</li>
  <li>Enable switching the theme</li>
</ul>
<div>
  <button class="btn">Dark</button>
</div>
```

- Add a button selector to the CSS code. Set the color and background-color properties in the button selector to make the button colors distinct from the general light or dark theme colors. This button-specific selector overrides the universal selector (*) used in your CSS file to apply font colors.

-

> Table 2.30
>
> .btn {
>
>   color: var(–btnFontColor);
>
>   background-color: var(–btnBg);
>
> }

- Add some rules for the button's height, form, appearance, and location next. The CSS below adds a circular button to the right of the page header.

Table 2.31

```css
.btn {
    position: absolute;
    top: 20px;
    left: 250px;
    height: 50px;
    width: 50px;
    border-radius: 50%;
    border: none;
    color: var(--btnFontColor);
    background-color: var(--btnBg);
}
```

- After the button selector, apply a pseudo-class selector, btn: focus, to change the button's appearance. When you set the outline-style rule to zero, you remove the rectangular outline that appears when the button is pressed (receives focus).

Table 2.32

.btn:focus { outline-style: none; }

- Following that, change the CSS for the light and dark themes. Create two new variables, btnFontColor and btnBg, to define the button's backdrop and font colors.

Table 2.33

.light-theme {

  –bg: var(–green);

  –fontColor: var(–black);

  –btnBg: var(–black);

  –btnFontColor: var(–white);

}

.dark-theme {

  –bg: var(–black);

  –fontColor: var(–green);

  –btnBg: var(–white);

  –btnFontColor: var(–black);

}

5. Add Event Holder

You will need an event handler in your JavaScript file to make the button do something when you push it. An event handler for the click event is required for a button. When the click event happens, the event handler function is called. You need a reference to the button before you can add the event handler.

- To get the button connection, use document.querySelector in your JavaScript file.

> **Table 2.34**
>
> const switcher = document.querySelector('.btn');

- Then, for the click event, add an event listener and an event controller. You add a listener for the click case in the following code. Your real event handler is the feature transferred through the event listener.

> **Table 2.35**
>
> switcher.addEventListener('click', function() {
>
> document.body.classList.toggle('dark-theme')
> });

You used the toggle method in the preceding code to shift the element's class to dark-theme. This allows the dark theme styles to be added instead of the light theme styles. However, the button label must also be changed to reflect the right theme, so you must have and if comment to verify the new theme and change the button label.

The full JavaScript code should look like this.

Table 2.36

```
'use strict'

const switcher = document.querySelector('.btn');

switcher.addEventListener('click', function() {

document.body.classList.toggle('dark-theme')

  var className = document.body.className;
  if(className == "light-theme") {
    this.textContent = "Dark";
  }
  else {
    this.textContent = "Light";
  }

});
```

Camel case is a JavaScript convention for variable names of more than one letter, such as the variable className.

6. Console Message

You can add a coded message that would not be shown on your website. What you type in the console, though, would be seen in the browser development features. Using console messages and see the outcome of the coding can be very useful.

- After the if expression, but inside the event listener, add a call to console.log.

Table 2.37

...

    console.log('current class name: ' + className);
});

When you are in a JavaScript file in Visual Studio Code, you can use autocomplete for console.log by typing log and then pressing Enter.

You may describe a text string by enclosing it in single or double-quotes.

7. Open in Browser

And if you were just modifying the app.js file, you could preview the changes by selecting the index.html file, as previously mentioned.

- To preview, right-click index.html and choose Open In Default Browser. The page will open in your default tab.
- To turn to the dark theme, click the new Dark button.

- Check that everything seems to be in order.

8. **Check Page in Developer Tools**

   - Open Developer Software.

   - In Edge, click the Developer Tools keyboard shortcut, F12 (FN+F12). Alternatively, click Alt+X and tap Developer Tools to display Settings and more.

   - In Chrome, click the Developer Tools keyboard shortcut, Option+Command+I. (F12 is also an option.)

   - Choose the Styles tab.

   - Choose the Elements tab.

   - Choose the <body> part. Examine the theme that has been added in the Styles tab. The dark-theme models are used if the existing theme is dull. Be certain that the dark theme is picked.

   - To view the screen, go to the console.log message, "current class name: light-theme dark-theme."

Using the console, you can see how **CSS** theme swapping is done in an amusing way. When you turn to the dark theme, both class names are added to the <body> part. However, the most recently applied class name, the dark theme, takes precedence. The dark theme rules bypass the light theme rules, as seen by the strikethrough text in the Styles column.

Here you go. You have built your website, accessorized it, and made it functional. Enjoy!

In the next chapters, you will learn to code your own games!

Chapter 4: Coding for Pong

Pong is a two-dimensional competition that is similar to table tennis. The player moves an in-game paddle vertically over the right or left side of the screen to bounce the ball back to the rival. The target is for one player to score eleven points before the other. Points are scored when the rival player fails to return the ball to the other.

The original Pong was played with two paddles to volley a small ball forward and backward on a screen. Ralph Baer, a German-born American television programmer, suggested creating basic video games that people could enjoy on their home television sets in 1958, laying the foundations for Pong.

Pong was the first commercially popular computer game. Along with the Magnavox Odyssey, it helped to develop the video game industry. Several developers started making games that closely resembled its gameplay soon after its publication. Eventually, Atari's rivals launched different forms of video games that differed from Pong's initial model to differing degrees, prompting Atari to urge its employees to look past Pong and create more creative games.

Now let me walk you through the step by step process of coding your own Pong using HTML, CSS, and JavaScript.

First of all, open,

www.codepen.io

Let's start with HTML.

4.1 HTML Code for Pong

HTML code is pretty short. Look below:

Table 3.1

```
<!DOCTYPE html>
<html>
 <head>
        <!- meta tags are not necessary here, but having
them always is a good practice ->
        <meta charset="UTF-8">
        <meta name="viewport" content="width=device-
width, initial-scale=1.0">
        <!- title ->
        <title>Ping Pong</title>
        <!- some css styles ->
        <style>
        * {
        padding: 0;
        margin: 0;
        }

        body {
        width: 100vw;
        height: 100vh;
        display: flex;
        justify-content: center;
        align-items: center;
        }
```

```
        </style>
    </head>
    <body>


        <!-- our "canvas" where we draw things-->
        <canvas id="canvas" width="600" height="400">


        </canvas>


        <!-- link to script.js -->
        <script type="text/javascript" src="app.js"></script>
    </body>
</html>
```

We will do most of the work in JavaScript.

4.2 CSS Code for Pong

Luckily, you don't need a CSS code to develop pong. So, let's move onto JavaScript.

4.3 JavaScript Code for Pong

JavaScript code for Pong is the real deal. Let's begin:

Table 3.2

```javascript
// grab a reference of our "canvas" using its id

const canvas = document.getElementById('canvas');

/* get a "context". Without "context", we can't draw on canvas */

const ctx = canvas.getContext('2d');


// some sounds

const hitSound = new Audio();

const scoreSound = new Audio();

const wallHitSound = new Audio();


hitSound.src = 'https://raw.githubusercontent.com/the-coding-pie/Ping-Pong-Javascript/master/sounds/hitSound.wav';

scoreSound.src = 'https://raw.githubusercontent.com/the-coding-pie/Ping-Pong-Javascript/master/sounds/scoreSound.wav';

wallHitSound.src =
```

```javascript
'https://raw.githubusercontent.com/the-coding-
pie/Ping-Pong-
Javascript/master/sounds/wallHitSound.wav';

/* some extra variables */
const netWidth = 4;
const netHeight = canvas.height;

const paddleWidth = 10;
const paddleHeight = 100;

let upArrowPressed = false;
let downArrowPressed = false;

/* some extra variables ends */

/* objects */
// net
const net = {
  x: canvas.width / 2 - netWidth / 2,
  y: 0,
  width: netWidth,
  height: netHeight,
  color: "#FFF"
};

// user paddle
```

```
const user = {
  x: 10,
  y: canvas.height / 2 - paddleHeight / 2,
  width: paddleWidth,
  height: paddleHeight,
  color: '#FFF',
  score: 0
};

const ai = {
  x: canvas.width - (paddleWidth + 10),
  y: canvas.height / 2 - paddleHeight / 2,
  width: paddleWidth,
  height: paddleHeight,
  color: '#FFF',
  score: 0
};

// ball
const ball = {
  x: canvas.width / 2,
  y: canvas.height / 2,
  radius: 7,
  speed: 7,
  velocityX: 5,
  velocityY: 5,
```

```javascript
  color: '#05EDFF'
};


/* objects declaration ends */


/* drawing functions */
// function to draw net
function drawNet() {
  // set the color of net
  ctx.fillStyle = net.color;

  // syntax -> fillRect(x, y, width, height)
  ctx.fillRect(net.x, net.y, net.width, net.height);
}


// function to draw score
function drawScore(x, y, score) {
  ctx.fillStyle = '#fff';
  ctx.font = '35px sans-serif';

  // syntax -> fillText(text, x, y)
  ctx.fillText(score, x, y);
}


// function to draw paddle
function drawPaddle(x, y, width, height, color) {
```

```javascript
  ctx.fillStyle = color;
  ctx.fillRect(x, y, width, height);
}


// function to draw ball
function drawBall(x, y, radius, color) {
  ctx.fillStyle = color;
  ctx.beginPath();
  // syntax -> arc(x, y, radius, startAngle,
endAngle, antiClockwise_or_not)
  ctx.arc(x, y, radius, 0, Math.PI * 2, true); // π *
2 Radians = 360 degrees
  ctx.closePath();
  ctx.fill();
}


/* drawing functions end */


/* moving Paddles */
// add an eventListener to browser window
window.addEventListener('keydown',
keyDownHandler);
window.addEventListener('keyup',
keyUpHandler);

// gets activated when we press down a key
function keyDownHandler(event) {
  // get the keyCode
```

```
switch (event.keyCode) {
    // "up arrow" key
    case 38:
    // set upArrowPressed = true
    upArrowPressed = true;
    break;
    // "down arrow" key
    case 40:
    downArrowPressed = true;
    break;
  }
}

// gets activated when we release the key
function keyUpHandler(event) {
  switch (event.keyCode) {
    // "up arraow" key
    case 38:
    upArrowPressed = false;
    break;
    // "down arrow" key
    case 40:
    downArrowPressed = false;
    break;
  }
}
```

```javascript
/* moving paddles section end */

// reset the ball
function reset() {
  // reset ball's value to older values
  ball.x = canvas.width / 2;
  ball.y = canvas.height / 2;
  ball.speed = 7;

  // changes the direction of ball
  ball.velocityX = -ball.velocityX;
  ball.velocityY = -ball.velocityY;
}

// collision Detect function
function collisionDetect(player, ball) {
  // returns true or false
  player.top = player.y;
  player.right = player.x + player.width;
  player.bottom = player.y + player.height;
  player.left = player.x;

  ball.top = ball.y - ball.radius;
  ball.right = ball.x + ball.radius;
  ball.bottom = ball.y + ball.radius;
```

```
    ball.left = ball.x - ball.radius;


    return ball.left < player.right && ball.top <
player.bottom && ball.right > player.left &&
ball.bottom > player.top;
}


// update function, to update things position
function update() {
  // move the paddle
  if (upArrowPressed && user.y > 0) {
      user.y -= 8;
  } else if (downArrowPressed && (user.y <
canvas.height - user.height)) {
      user.y += 8;
  }


  // check if ball hits top or bottom wall
  if (ball.y + ball.radius >= canvas.height ||
ball.y - ball.radius <= 0) {
      // play wallHitSound
      wallHitSound.play();
      ball.velocityY = -ball.velocityY;
  }


  // if ball hit on right wall
  if (ball.x + ball.radius >= canvas.width) {
      // play scoreSound
```

```javascript
        scoreSound.play();
        // then user scored 1 point
        user.score += 1;
        reset();
    }


    // if ball hit on left wall
    if (ball.x - ball.radius <= 0) {
        // play scoreSound
        scoreSound.play();
        // then ai scored 1 point
        ai.score += 1;
        reset();
    }


    // move the ball
    ball.x += ball.velocityX;
    ball.y += ball.velocityY;


    // ai paddle movement
    ai.y += ((ball.y - (ai.y + ai.height / 2))) * 0.09;


    // collision detection on paddles
    let player = (ball.x < canvas.width / 2) ? user :
ai;


    if (collisionDetect(player, ball)) {
```

```javascript
// play hitSound
hitSound.play();
// default angle is 0deg in Radian
let angle = 0;


// if ball hit the top of paddle
if (ball.y < (player.y + player.height / 2)) {
// then -1 * Math.PI / 4 = -45deg
angle = -1 * Math.PI / 4;
} else if (ball.y > (player.y + player.height /
2)) {
// if it hit the bottom of paddle
// then angle will be Math.PI / 4 = 45deg
angle = Math.PI / 4;
}


/* change velocity of ball according to on
which paddle the ball hitted */
ball.velocityX = (player === user ? 1 : -1) *
ball.speed * Math.cos(angle);
ball.velocityY        =        ball.speed        *
Math.sin(angle);

// increase ball speed
ball.speed += 0.2;
}
}
```

```javascript
// render function draws everything on to canvas
function render() {
  // set a style
  ctx.fillStyle = "#000"; /* whatever comes below
  this acquires black color (#000). */
  // draws the black board
  ctx.fillRect(0, 0, canvas.width, canvas.height);


  // draw net
  drawNet();
  // draw user score
  drawScore(canvas.width / 4, canvas.height / 6,
  user.score);
  // draw ai score
  drawScore(3 * canvas.width / 4, canvas.height /
  6, ai.score);
  // draw user paddle
  drawPaddle(user.x,      user.y,      uscr.width,
  user.height, user.color);
  // draw ai paddle
  drawPaddle(ai.x,   ai.y,   ai.width,   ai.height,
  ai.color);
  // draw ball
  drawBall(ball.x, ball.y, ball.radius, ball.color);
}


// gameLoop
function gameLoop() {
```

```
    // update() function here
    update();
    // render() function here
    render();
}


// calls gameLoop() function 60 times per
second
setInterval(gameLoop, 1000 / 60);
```

Now enjoy playing pong!

4.4 Results of Pong

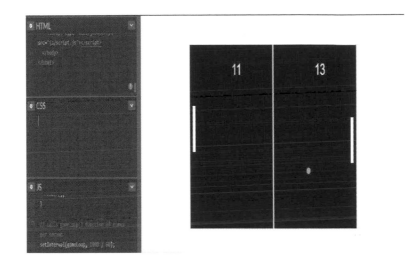

Chapter 5: Coding for Rock, Paper, and Scissors

Rock, Paper, and Scissors is usually taught to children in helping them solve disputes between themselves without parental interference. It is thought to be a game of chance that relies on pure luck, equivalent to tossing coins or drawing straws.

The game works using three potential hand signals: paper, scissors and rock. The paper is a flat hand. Moreover, here the palm is down and the thumb is extended. The rock is a clenched fist. The scissors is a fist. Here, the middle and index fingers are completely extended in the direction of the opponent. Paper triumphs over rock. Rock triumphs over scissors. Scissors triumph over paper. If all players make the same gesture with their hands, the game is declared a draw, and play continues before a definite winner is determined. Both players send their hand signs at the same time.

Finger-flashing sports like this game have been believed to exist since prehistoric times, but the game's origins are unknown. The oldest registered reference was found in a tomb at Egypt's Beni Hasan burial site as a wall painting. It dates back to about 2000 B.C. The game was discovered on a Japanese scroll, centuries later. The game is played in cultures all over the globe. It is also widely played in Japan. It is known there as Jan Ken Pon or Jan-Ken.

Now let me help you code your own Rock, Paper, and Scissors using HTML, CSS, and JavaScript.

First of all, open,

www.codepen.io

Let's begin with HTML.

5.1 HTML Code for Rock, Paper, and Scissors

The HTML code for this game goes as follows:

Table 4.4

```html
<!DOCTYPE html>
<html lang="en">
<head>

<meta charset="UTF-8">

<meta name="viewport" content="width=device-width,
initial-scale=1.0">

<title>R-P-S Game</title>

<link rel="stylesheet" href="style.css">

<script
src="https://kit.fontawesome.com/e391ce7786.js"
crossorigin="anonymous"></script>

<script src="app.js" defer></script>
</head>
<body>

<h1>Rock Paper Scissors</h1>

<h2 id="demo">Try your luck ! </h2>

<div class="container">
```

I will now move onto CSS.

5.2 CSS Code for Rock, Paper, and Scissors

The CSS code goes as follows:

Table 4.2

```
*{

margin: 0;

padding: 0;
```

You can now move onto the final step.

5.3 Java Script Code for Rock, Paper, and Scissors

You can follow the code below:

Table 4.3

```javascript
let computerScore = 1;

let playerScore = 1;

const pScore = document.getElementById('playerScore');

const cScore = document.getElementById('computerScore');

const buttons = document.querySelectorAll('.selection button');

const showIcon = document.querySelector('.show i');

const computerShowIcon = document.querySelector('.computer i');


const randomClasses = ["fas fa-hand-rock", "fas fa-hand-paper","fas fa-hand-scissors"];

const text = document.getElementById('demo');

const text2 = document.getElementById('demo2');


// Game Functionality.
const game = () =>{


buttons.forEach(btn =>{


btn.addEventListener('click',(e)=>{


// Random rock paper scissor for the computer and clicked ones for the player

let clickedBtn = e.target.className;
```

There you have your own "Rock, Paper and Scissors" game.

5.4 Results of Rock, Paper, Scissors

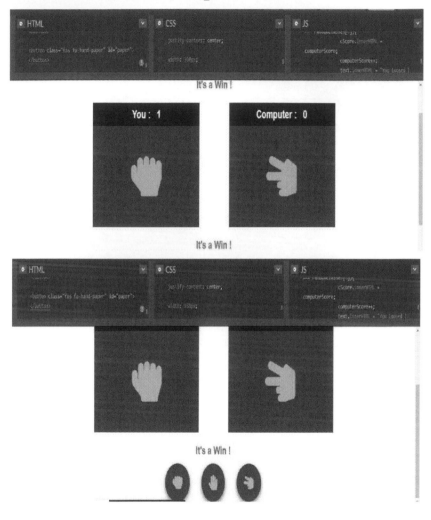

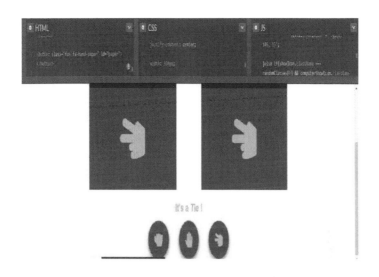

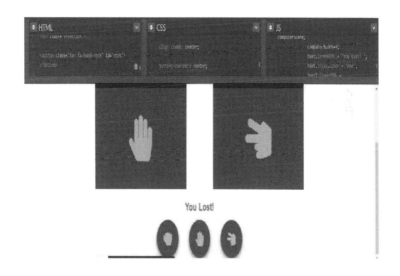

Chapter 6: Coding 4 Snake

Snake is basically a video game that first appeared in arcades during the late 1970s and has since become a classic. Gremlin Industries developed and distributed it in 1976. The same year, it was cloned as Bigfoot Bonkers. In 1998, it came out on Nokia phones as a default pre-loaded game. The player is given a thin long snake-like creature that roams around in a bordered screen. It has to collect food (or other items) while avoiding touching the edges of the playing space or bumping into its own tail. The snake's tail grows with each bite of food. It makes the game more challenging. The direction of the head of the snake (down, up, right, left) is regulated by the owner, and the body of the snake follows. The target is to score as high as you can, not touching the border of the screen or its own tail.

Now let me explain how you can code your own "Snake." You won't need any CSS code to develop this game.

First of all, open,

www.codepen.io

Let's get into it.

6.1 HTML Code for Snake

Follow the codes below:

```
Table 5.1
<!doctype html>
<html lang="en">
  <head>
  <!- Required meta tags ->
  <meta charset="utf-8">
  <meta name="viewport" content="width=device-width, initial-scale=1, shrink-to-fit=no">
```

<!-- Bootstrap CSS -->

```
Table 5.2

<link                    rel="stylesheet"
href="https://stackpath.bootstrapcdn.com/bootstra
p/4.3.1/css/bootstrap.min.css"    integrity="sha384-
ggOyR0iXCbMQv3Xipma34MD+dH/1fQ784/j6c
Y/iJTQUOhcWr7x9JvoRxT2MZw1T"
crossorigin="anonymous">


<title>Hello, world!</title>

</head>

<body    class="container   w-100   mx-auto   text-
center">

<h1>Use  the  arrow  keys  and  refresh  to  play
again!</h1>

<div>

<canvas class="mx-auto bg-dark p-0 m-0 img-fluid"
id='c'></canvas>

</div>
```

<!-- Optional JavaScript -->

```
Table 5.3

<!-- jQuery first, then Popper.js, then Bootstrap JS -->

<script src="https://code.jquery.com/jquery-
3.3.1.slim.min.js" integrity="sha384-
q8i/X+965DzO0rT7abK41JStQIAqVgRVzpbzo5sm
XKp4YfRvH+8abtTE1Pi6jizo"
crossorigin="anonymous"></script>

<script
src="https://cdnjs.cloudflare.com/ajax/libs/popper.js/1.
14.7/umd/popper.min.js" integrity="sha384-
UO2eT0CpHqdSJQ6hJty5KVphtPhzWj9WO1clHT
MGa3JDZwrnQq4sF86dIHNDz0W1"
crossorigin="anonymous"></script>

<script
src="https://stackpath.bootstrapcdn.com/bootstrap/4.3
.1/js/bootstrap.min.js" integrity="sha384-
JjSmVgyd0p3pXB1rRibZUAYoIIy6OrQ6VrjIEaFf/n
JGzIxFDsf4x0xIM+B07jRM"
crossorigin="anonymous"></script>

</body>

</html>
```

Let's move onto Javascript.

6.2 JavaScript Code for Snake

Table 5.4

```javascript
(function() {

  var SIZE = 500; // Size of the play-field in pixels

  var GRID_SIZE = SIZE / 50;

  var c = document.getElementById('c');

  c.height = c.width = SIZE * 2; // 2x our resolution so retina screens look good

  c.style.width = c.style.height = SIZE + 'px';

  var context = c.getContext('2d');

  context.scale(2, 2); // Scale our canvas for retina screens


  var direction = newDirection = 1; // -2: up, 2: down, -1: left, 1: right

  var snakeLength = 5;

  var snake = [{x: SIZE / 2, y: SIZE / 2}]; // Snake starts in the center

  var candy = null;

  var end = false;


  function randomOffset() {
  return Math.floor(Math.random() * SIZE / GRID_SIZE) * GRID_SIZE;
  }


  function stringifyCoord(obj) {
  return [obj.x, obj.y].join(',');
  }
```

There you have your "Snake" game!

6.3 Results of Snake

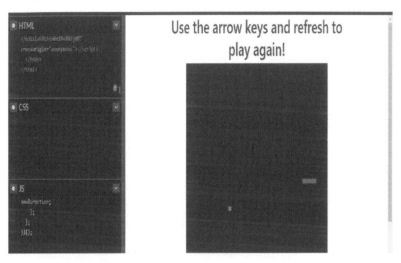

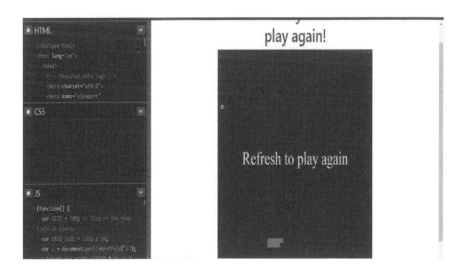

Chapter 7: Coding for Tic Tac Toe

Tic Tac Toe is a famous game in which two people alternatively place Os and Xs in square compartments of a diagram created by two horizontal lines overlapping two vertical lines, each attempting to obtain a row of 3 Os or 3 Xs before the rival.

Around the 1st century B.C., an early version of the game was played in the Roman Empire. It was known as terni lapilli. It translates as "three pebbles at a time." Grid marks from the game have been found all over Roman ruins. Ancient Egyptian ruins have also yielded evidence of the game.

Now let me help you code your own Tic Tac Toe using HTML, CSS, and JavaScript.

First of all, open,

www.codepen.io

Let's start with HTML.

7.1 HTML Code for Tic Tac Toe

HTML code for this simple game goes as follows:

Table 6.1

```html
<html lang="en">
  <head>
    <meta charset="utf-8">
    <meta name="viewport" content="width=device-width, initial-scale=1.0">

    <title>Tic-tac-toe</title>
    <link href="https://fonts.googleapis.com/css?family=Indie+Flower" rel="stylesheet">
  </head>
  <body onload="initialize()">

    <h1>Tic—Tac—Toe</h1>
    <table id="table_game">

      <tr><td class="td_game"><div id="cell0" onclick="cellClicked(this.id)" class="fixed"></div></td><td class="td_game"><div id="cell1" onclick="cellClicked(this.id)" class="fixed"></div></td><td class="td_game"><div id="cell2" onclick="cellClicked(this.id)" class="fixed"></div></td></tr>

      <tr><td class="td_game"><div id="cell3" onclick="cellClicked(this.id)" class="fixed"></div></td><td class="td_game"><div id="cell4" onclick="cellClicked(this.id)"
```

Let's move onto CSS.

7.2 CSS Code for Tic Tac Toe

You can proceed in the following manner in CSS for Tic Tac Toe code:

```
Table 6.2
body {

background-color: rgb(32, 32, 32);

background-image:
url("https://janschreiber.github.io/img2/black-chalk.jpg");
    color: rgb(230, 230, 230);
    text-align: center;
    font-family: 'Indie Flower', 'Comic Sans', cursive;
    font-size: 0.7em;
}
h1 {
    line-height: 1em;
    margin-bottom: 0;
    padding-bottom: 5px;
    font-size: 2.8em;
    font-weight: bold;
}
h2 {
```

```css
    font-size: 1.3em;

    font-weight: bold;

    padding: 0;

    margin: 0;


}
h3 {

    font-size: 1.1em;


text-decoration: underline;


text-decoration-style: dashed;

    padding: 0;

    margin: 10px 0 2px 0;

}
table {

    margin: 2% auto;


border-collapse: collapse;

}
#table_game {

    position: relative;

    font-size: 120px;

    margin: 1% auto;


border-collapse: collapse;
```

```css
}
.td_game {
    border: 4px solid rgb(230, 230, 230);
    width: 90px;
    height: 90px;
    padding: 0;
    vertical-align: middle;
    text-align: center;
}
.fixed {
    width: 90px;
    height: 90px;
    line-height: 90px;
    display: block;
    overflow: hidden;
    cursor: pointer;
}
.td_list {
    text-align: center;
    font-size: 1.3em;
    font-weight: bold;
}
.th_list {
    font-size: 1.3em;
    font-weight: bold;
    text-align: center;
```

```css
    text-decoration: underline;
}
#restart {
    font-size: 3em;
    width: 1em;
    height: 0.9em;
    cursor: pointer;
    margin: 0 auto;
    overflow: hidden;
}
.x {
    color: darksalmon;
    position: relative;
    top: -8px;
    font-size: 1.2em;
    cursor: default;
}
.o {
    color: aquamarine;
    position: relative;
    top: -7px;
    font-size: 1.0em;
    cursor: default;
}
/* modal background */
```

```css
.modal {
    display: none;
    position: fixed;
    z-index: 1;
    left: 0;
    top: 0;
    width: 100%;
    height: 100%;
    overflow: auto; /* enable scroll if needed */

background-color: black; /* fallback color */

background-color: rgba(0, 0, 0, 0.6);
}

/* modal content */
.modal-content {

background-color: rgb(240, 240, 240);
    color: rgb(32, 32, 32);
    font-size: 2em;
    font-weight: bold;
    /* 16 % from the top and centered */
    margin: 16% auto;
    padding: 20px;
    border: 2px solid black;
```

```css
    border-radius: 10px;
    width: 380px;
    max-width: 80%;
}
.modal-content p {
    margin: 0;
    padding: 0;
}

/* close button for modal dialog */
.close {
    color: rgb(170, 170, 170);
    float: right;
    position: relative;
    top: -25px;
    right: -10px;
    font-size: 34px;
    font-weight: bold;
}
.close:hover,
.close:focus {
    color: black;

text-decoration: none;
    cursor: pointer;
}
```

```
.win-color {

background-color: rgb(240, 240, 240);
}
```

It is time to move onto the last step.

7.3 JavaScript Code for Tic Tac Toe

For the final step of coding Tic Tac Toe you can follow the code below:

```
Table 6.3
"use strict";
// Bind Esc key to closing the modal dialog
document.onkeypress = function (evt) {
    evt = evt || window.event;
    var modal =
document.getElementsByClassName("modal")[0];
    if (evt.keyCode === 27) {

modal.style.display = "none";
    }
};


// When the user clicks somewhere outside the
modal dialog, close it
window.onclick = function (evt) {
    var modal =
document.getElementsByClassName("modal")[0];
    if (evt.target === modal) {

modal.style.display = "none";
    }
};
```

// HELPER FUNCTIONS

```
Table 6.4
function sumArray(array) {
   var sum = 0,
      i = 0;
   for (i = 0; i < array.length; i++) {
      sum += array[i];
   }
   return sum;
}

function isInArray(element, array) {
   if (array.indexOf(element) > -1) {
      return true;
   }
   return false;
}

function shuffleArray(array) {
   var counter = array.length,
      temp,
      index;
   while (counter > 0) {
      index   =   Math.floor(Math.random()   *
counter);
      counter-;
```

```
        temp = array[counter];
        array[counter] = array[index];
        array[index] = temp;
    }
    return array;
}


function intRandom(min, max) {
    var rand = min + Math.random() * (max + 1 - min);
    return Math.floor(rand);
}
```

// GLOBAL VARIABLES

Table 6.5

```javascript
var moves = 0,
    winner = 0,
    x = 1,
    o = 3,
    player = x,
    computer = o,
    whoseTurn = x,
    gameOver = false,
    score = {
        ties: 0,
        player: 0,
        computer: 0
    },
    xText              =              "<span
class=\"x\">&times;</class>",
    oText = "<span class=\"o\">o</class>",
    playerText = xText,
    computerText = oText,
    difficulty = 1,
    myGrid = null;
```

```
//------------------------------------
// GRID OBJECT
//------------------------------------
```

// Grid constructor

```
Table 6.6
function Grid() {
    this.cells = new Array(9);
}
```

// Grid methods

```
Table 6.7
// Get free cells in an array.
// Returns an array of indices in the original Grid.cells array, not the values
// of the array elements.
// Their values can be accessed as Grid.cells[index].
Grid.prototype.getFreeCellIndices = function () {
    var i = 0,
        resultArray = [];
    for (i = 0; i < this.cells.length; i++) {
        if (this.cells[i] === 0) {

resultArray.push(i);
```

```
        }
    }
    //          console.log("resultArray:          "          +
resultArray.toString());
    // debugger;
    return resultArray;
};


// Get a row (accepts 0, 1, or 2 as argument).
// Returns the values of the elements.
Grid.prototype.getRowValues = function (index) {
    if (index !== 0 && index !== 1 && index !== 2) {

console.error("Wrong arg for getRowValues!");
        return undefined;
    }
    var i = index * 3;
    return this.cells.slice(i, i + 3);
};


// Get a row (accepts 0, 1, or 2 as argument).
// Returns an array with the indices, not their values.
Grid.prototype.getRowIndices = function (index) {
    if (index !== 0 && index !== 1 && index !== 2) {

console.error("Wrong arg for getRowIndices!");
        return undefined;
```

```javascript
    }
    var row = [];
    index = index * 3;
    row.push(index);
    row.push(index + 1);
    row.push(index + 2);
    return row;
};


// get a column (values)
Grid.prototype.getColumnValues = function (index)
{
    if (index !== 0 && index !== 1 && index !== 2) {

console.error("Wrong arg for getColumnValues!");
        return undefined;
    }
    var i, column = [];
    for (i = index; i < this.cells.length; i += 3) {

column.push(this.cells[i]);
    }
    return column;
};

// get a column (indices)
Grid.prototype.getColumnIndices = function (index)
```

```
{
    if (index !== 0 && index !== 1 && index !== 2) {

console.error("Wrong arg for getColumnIndices!");
        return undefined;
    }
    var i, column = [];
    for (i = index; i < this.cells.length; i += 3) {

column.push(i);
    }
    return column;
};

// get diagonal cells
// arg 0: from top-left
// arg 1: from top-right
Grid.prototype.getDiagValues = function (arg) {
    var cells = [];
    if (arg !== 1 && arg !== 0) {

console.error("Wrong arg for getDiagValues!");
        return undefined;
    } else if (arg === 0) {
        cells.push(this.cells[0]);
```

```javascript
cells.push(this.cells[4]);

cells.push(this.cells[8]);
    } else {

cells.push(this.cells[2]);

cells.push(this.cells[4]);

cells.push(this.cells[6]);
    }
    return cells;
};

// get diagonal cells
// arg 0: from top-left
// arg 1: from top-right
Grid.prototype.getDiagIndices = function (arg) {
    if (arg !== 1 && arg !== 0) {

console.error("Wrong arg for getDiagIndices!");
        return undefined;
    } else if (arg === 0) {
        return [0, 4, 8];
    } else {
        return [2, 4, 6];
```

```
        }
};


// Get first index with two in a row (accepts computer
or player as argument)

Grid.prototype.getFirstWithTwoInARow = function
(agent) {

    if (agent !== computer && agent !== player) {

        console.error("Function
getFirstWithTwoInARow accepts only player or
computer as argument.");

        return undefined;

    }

    var sum = agent * 2,

        freeCells                              =
shuffleArray(this.getFreeCellIndices());

    for (var i = 0; i < freeCells.length; i++) {

        for (var j = 0; j < 3; j++) {

            var rowV = this.getRowValues(j);

            var rowI = this.getRowIndices(j);

            var colV = this.getColumnValues(j);

            var colI = this.getColumnIndices(j);

            if    (sumArray(rowV)    ==    sum    &&
isInArray(freeCells[i], rowI)) {

                return freeCells[i];

            } else if (sumArray(colV) == sum &&
isInArray(freeCells[i], colI)) {

                return freeCells[i];
```

```
        }
    }
    for (j = 0; j < 2; j++) {
        var diagV = this.getDiagValues(j);
        var diagI = this.getDiagIndices(j);
        if    (sumArray(diagV)    ==    sum    &&
isInArray(freeCells[i], diagI)) {
            return freeCells[i];
        }
    }
    }
    return false;
};


Grid.prototype.reset = function () {
    for (var i = 0; i < this.cells.length; i++) {
        this.cells[i] = 0;
    }
    return true;
};
```

// MAIN FUNCTIONS

Table 6.8

```javascript
// executed when the page loads
function initialize() {
    myGrid = new Grid();
    moves = 0;
    winner = 0;
    gameOver = false;
    whoseTurn = player; // default, this may change
    for (var i = 0; i <= myGrid.cells.length - 1; i++) {

myGrid.cells[i] = 0;
    }
    // setTimeout(assignRoles, 500);

setTimeout(showOptions, 500);
    // debugger;
}


// Ask player if they want to play as X or O. X goes first.
function assignRoles() {
    askUser("Do you want to go first?");

document.getElementById("yesBtn").addEventListener(
"click", makePlayerX);


document.getElementById("noBtn").addEventListener(
"click", makePlayerO);
```

That is it!

Enjoy your first game!

7.4 Results of Tic Tac Toe

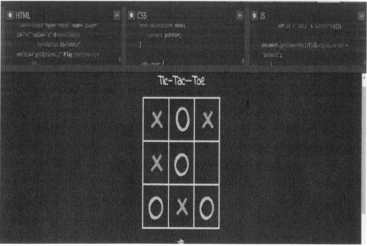

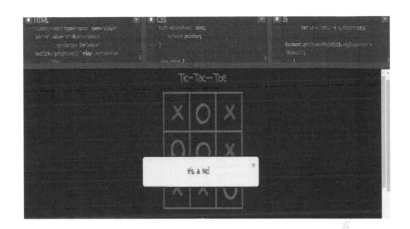

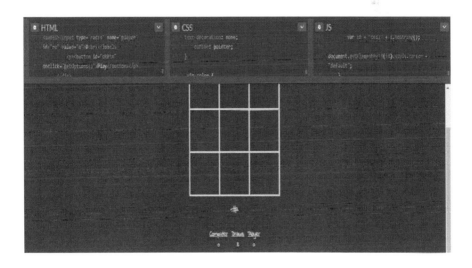

Chapter 8: Coding for Dinosaurs

Chrome Dino is a straightforward endless runner in which you leap over cacti and duck under obstacles. When you attempt to access a website while disconnected from the Internet, the dinosaur game emerges.

The Chrome dino game was developed by Google design team members Sebastien Gabriel, Edward Jung, and Alan Bettes. The prehistoric style was intentional, according to Chrome artist Sebastien Gabriel. In early 2014, the concept of an 'endless racer' as an Easter egg inside the 'you're-offline' page was born." It is a play on returning to the 'prehistoric period,' where there was no Wi-Fi. The game will award you a maximum score of 99999 before resetting to 0.

The Chrome Dino game has amazing figures, particularly for something that is often hidden from view and is only likely to appear if your Internet goes down. According to a Chrome UX engineer, Edward Jung, 270 million games are played per month through desktop and mobile platforms.

Now let me explain how you can code your own "Dino" using HTML and JavaScript. You will not need CSS for Dino.

First of all, open,

www.codepen.io

For The Dino game, you do not need any HTML code. Let's start with CSS.

8.1 CSS Code for Dino

The code goes as follows:

Table 7.1

```
Canvas
{
    margin: auto;
    position: absolute;
    top: 0;
    left: 0;
    bottom: 0;
    right: 0;
}
```

You can now move onto the final step, aka. JavaScript.

8.2 JavaScript Code for Dino

```
Table 7.2
var speed;
var y;
var yVelocity;
var onGround;

var score;
var highscore;

var horizon;
var obstacles = [];

function setup()
{
  createCanvas(600, 200);

  textAlign(CENTER);

  horizon = height - 40;
  y = 20;
  score = highscore = yVelocity = 0;
  speed = 6;
  onGround = false;
}
```

```
function draw()
{
  background(51);

  //draw horizon
  stroke(255);
  line(0, horizon, width, horizon);

  fill('#999');
  ellipse(40, y, 40);

  if(frameCount % 120 === 0)
  {
    speed *= 1.05;
  }
  if(frameCount % 30 === 0)
  {
    var n = noise(frameCount);
    if(n>0.5)
    {
      newObstacles(n);
    }
  }
  score++;
  textSize(20);
```

```
        text("Score : " + score, width / 2, 30);


    updateObstacles();
    handleTRex();
}


function updateObstacles()
{
    for(var i = obstacles.length - 1; i >= 0; i--)
    {
        obstacles[i].x -= speed;
        var x = obstacles[i].x;
        var size = obstacles[i].size;
        var s2 = size / 2;
        if(x > -30)
        {
                //if it's on screen
            fill(obstacles[i].color);
                rect(x, horizon - size, size, size);
                var x1 = x + s2;
                var y1 = horizon - s2;
                if(dist(x1, y1, 40, y) < s2 + 20)
                {
                //collision
            textAlign(CENTER);
            textSize(40);
```

```
            text("Game Over", width/2, height/2);

            textSize(20);

            text("Press    F5    to    restart",    width/2,
height/2 + 40);

                noLoop();

            //restart();

                }

    }

    else

    {

            //delete from array

        obstacles.splice(i, 1);

    }

    }

}


//function restart()

//{

//                if(mouseIsPressed                ||
keyIsDown(UP_ARROW) || keyIsDown(32))

    // {

    //   draw();

    // }

//}


function Obstacles(r, c)

{
```

```
    this.x = 620;
    this.size = r;
    this.color = c;
}


function newObstacles(n)
{
    var     obs    =    new    Obstacles(n*50,
    color(random(255),              random(255),
    random(255)));

    obstacles.push(obs);
}


function handleTRex()
{
  if( y+20+yVelocity < horizon )
    {
    yVelocity += map(frameCount, 0, 3600, 0.7,
2);
    onGround = false;
    }
  else
    {
    yVelocity = 0;
    onGround = true;
    }
  if(mouseIsPressed                              ||
```

```
keyIsDown(UP_ARROW) || keyIsDown(32))
  {
  if(onGround)
    {
        yVelocity -= map(frameCount, 0,
3600, 9, 15);
        onGround = false;
        }
    }
  y += yVelocity;
  }
```

That is all kids. You have your Dino game!

8.3 Results of Dino

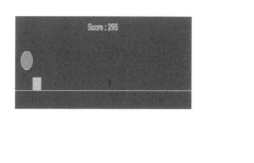

Chapter 9: Coding Exercise – Test Yourself

I am hopeful that you have developed a good understanding of the major coding languages. Building your own website and practicing code on games must have helped you understand concepts better. In this last chapter, I want to provide you with some exercises, so that your grasp on coding becomes stronger. I will include exercises for HTML, CSS, and JavaScript step by step.

9.1 HTML Exercises

Here you go:

- Create a website that displays the numbers from 1 to 10 on the desktop.

- Make a website that displays your name on the screen.

- Make a website with the title "Your Favorite Color Name."

- Make a webpage that displays any text you want on the screen. Do not include the head section in your code.

- Make a website that displays the message "Do you know when this website was made? The answer can be found in the page's title on the screen. Change the page's title to the current date.

- Display the squares of 1-20. Each number must be on its own line, with the number 2 written next to it, followed by an equal sign, and finally the result. (For instance, 102 = 100.)

- Using the   command, print two paragraphs that are both indented.

- Print ten names. They should have a line break between them. Alphabetize the list. Add a subscripted number in front of each name. It should be based on where it will appear in the organized list. (Alan1 is an example.) Print the un-alphabetized list first, including the subscript number in front of each name, followed by the organized list. An <h1> level heading should be used for both lists.

- Make two lists of vegetables and fruits. You must create one list as numbered, while the other should not be numbered.

- Print a piece of preformatted text by your own choice. (Tip: use the <pre> tag)

- Print, an h1 heading. It should be followed by a 100 percent width horizontal line. Display a paragraph related to the text under the heading below this line.

- Print both a short and a long quotation. Each quote should be attributed to its source.

- Print a 5-item definition list.

- Print ten different abbreviations and acronyms, each separated by two lines. Signify the information that acronyms and abbreviations represent.

- Print two addresses on the top of the envelopes in the same format (put the receiver's address in the center and sender's address in the left corner at the top.)

- Write your name in red.

- Tahoma font is used to print the name.

- Display the numbers 1 through 10. No number should have the same color.

- Print a paragraph of four or five words. Each sentence should be written in a different font.

- Print your name on the phone. No letter should have the same heading size.

- Print a paragraph that is a book review, including the title and name. Name and tittle should be italicized and made bold.

- Show five distinct images. Between each picture, skip two lines. Each picture should be labeled with a title.

- Show a picture that will take you to a search engine of your choosing when tapped. (should be opened in a new window).

- Show a picture with a border scale of 2, a height of 200, and a width of 200.

- Show an icon that links to itself and displays the image in the tab on its own when tapped.

- Make four links to separate pages on four different websites, each of which should be open in a new browser.

- Make some links to different search engines (Google, Yahoo, Lycos, etc.)

- Create a page which should have a link in the center at top. When tapped, it should take you to the bottom of the page.

- Make a page with a link at the bottom of the page. When tapped, it should take you to the top of the page.

It is time for some CSS exercises.

9.2 CSS Exercises

Here we go:

- Assume that you are developing a website for recipes. A recipe has an ingredient list, a description, and a section with instructions. Create a website with a recipe for cheese sandwiches with tomato and bacon. The products should be shown in an unordered list with no pointers. Meat ingredients must have a dark green background color, vegetables a light red background, and dairy products a light blue background. The title must be in Helvetica font, and the instructions must have the "Instructions' ' heading with italic font.

- Add a CSS rule and correct HTML to style the backdrop of every other line of the unordered list with a light pink color. Using the RGB process, specify the background color.

- Create a two-column web page. Each column can take up half the page's width. The background on the left should be light brown, and the background on the right should be light grey. The half on the left should include a list of your top five athletes or celebrities, and the right should include the top six best-sellers in the Kindle store of Amazon in form of a list.

- Using the representation of the playing card, apply transformations and animations to make the card spin indefinitely.

- Create a navigation bar for the top of a webpage using the navigation feature. Include at least four links to the navigation bar using an unordered list shown inline in place of a block. Create the navigation bar's background light purple, but edit the title's background to dark purple when the cursor is moved over it.

- Create a web page in honor of someone you appreciate in your life. It just requires a basic understanding of CSS and HTML. Create a website about that user, including a picture of him or her. Add the person's picture and name to the top of the list, and then have a layout for the rest of the information below that. To give it a nice look, you can use CSS to add lists, paragraphs, links, and photos. For your website, use an appropriate background color and font type.

- Using embedded CSS, inline CSS, and external CSS, develop a webpage that shows "Hello You!" with font size 19 pixels, green color font, bold format, and "Times New Roman" font.

- Make a website that includes a link to each subject of your academic session. When a user clicks a tag, the page for that subject should be opened. (Please keep in mind that the topic pages can be left blank.) On hyperlinks, use CSS pseudo groups.

- Make a webpage that shows the class schedule and add the following effects to the table:

  Ø Display day names e.g. Mon, Tue etc. in bold, with the first letter of the day name in capital letters.

  Ø Use pink as the primary color for the table header and brown for the text in the table header.

  Ø Display lunch time in a significantly larger font than the rest of the text.

It is time for JavaScript exercises.

9.3 JavaScript Exercises

Here we go:

- Create a JavaScript program that prints the current window's contents.

- Create a JavaScript program that displays the current date and time in the format shown below.

    Ø Output Sample: It is Tuesday.

    Current time: 11 P.M. 40: 36

- Create a JavaScript program to calculate the area of a triangle whose three sides have lengths of 6, 7, and 8.

- Create a JavaScript program that shows the current date.

    Ø Output Expected: mm/dd/yyyy, dd-mm-yyyy

- Create a JavaScript code that rotates the string 'w3lresource' in the correct direction by deleting one letter from the ending of the string and adding it to the front on a regular basis.

- Create a JavaScript program to determine if the 1st of January is a Sunday between 2014 and 2050.

- Create a JavaScript program to decide when a given year in the Gregorian calendar is a leap year.

- Create a JavaScript code that takes an integer randomly from 1 to 10, then prompts the user to enter 1 guess number. If the input made by the user matches the guess number, your program should show the message "Good Work," otherwise, the message "Not matched" will be shown.

- Build a variable with a user-defined name using a JavaScript exercise.

- Create a JavaScript program to retrieve the web site's URL (loading page).

- Create a JavaScript code to calculate the sum of the two integers given. If the two values are the same, return three times their sum.

- Create a JavaScript program that removes a character from a given string at the stated location and returns the new string.

- Create a JavaScript program that checks two numbers and returns true if one of them is 50, or their total is 50.

- Create a JavaScript program that compares two properties to see if the first has equal property values to the second.

- Create a JavaScript program that translates a given number to a digit sequence.

- Create a JavaScript program that will copy a string to the clipboard.

- Create a JavaScript program to find the largest of three integers given.

- Create a JavaScript program that capitalizes the first letter of each word in a string.

Cheers, young learners!

Conclusion

It is not an overstatement that coding is the modern world's DNA. To function any website, phone app, computer software, and even several kitchen appliances depend on coding. This is why coders play such an important role in defining the digital era and the future.

In a general sense, learning to code is similar to learning any language – or, to be more precise, a family of languages. There are overarching guidelines that all scripts must adhere to. Also there are very specific rules for each script.

It is estimated that there is a significant shortage in the number of computer science graduates qualified to fill vacant coding positions. This represents the spread of coding across a variety of sectors. Indeed, computer sciences are becoming a critical component in a wide range of fields, including banking and medicine, where understanding of programming and coding is becoming increasingly relevant and important.

New markets are opening up opportunities for those seeking a career in computer sciences. Aside from the apparent examples of physicists, IT staff, designers and artists, engineers, and data aanalyst, opportunities in industries such as manufacturing and finance are starting to emerge. This means that coders are in high demand and are frequently well compensated financially.

This book helps you familiarize yourself with coding, and if you want, it can turn into a profitable career or even a fun hobby. Knowledge of coding is admirable and truly useful even if you do not pursue a career in it. It will be seen as a plus point. You will not only be prioritized as a job applicant, but also it will help you to communicate with your team effectively.

The first chapter helps you understand the concept of coding. Then, it mentions the perks of learning to code as earning profitability, smarter perspective, better job opportunities, improved creativity, effective communication and math skills, etc. Furthermore, internet sources for learning coding are jotted down.

In the second portion of the chapter, you got to know about the terminology to help you understand the rest of the book. Lastly, the top five programming languages like Java, JavaScript, HTML, CSS, and Python were explained with real-life applications.

The second chapter taught you to create your first basic webpage using HTML and CSS. It has a detailed description of HTML and CSS to help you do that. The content included the basic syntax and features with examples to show their usage. By the end of this chapter, you would have created the basic structure of your website with HTML and styled it through CSS.

The third chapter helped you add interactivity to your website through JavaScript. It included a detailed description of JavaScript with basic syntax and features with examples.

The rest of the five chapters taught you to code your own games. Tic Tac Toe, Rock, Paper, Scissors, Dino, snake, and pong were the games included. Each chapter has been dedicated to a single game.

The last chapter consisted of exercises related to HTML, CSS, and JavaScript for your practice.

The takeaway I wish you to have from this book is that coding is essential to learn whatever career you opt for, and it can be a fun activity when guided right. My intention for writing this book is to be the right guide for you.

I urge you to practice and practice using the knowledge given in this book, and I am sure you will become an amicable coder.

If you genuinely liked this book and it helped you in your coding journey, do not forget to leave a review on Amazon.

Here's to my young coders!

Printed in Great Britain
by Amazon